Sam George, Miriam Adeney, Chris ‸ [barcode] most important issues facing the glc [barcode]
They humanize refugees by telling their stories and offer a biblical, but clarion call to the church. Jesus was a refugee. He calls us to welcome the stranger. When we do, we welcome God. *Refugee Diaspora* is an urgent, poignant, and personal book. I couldn't commend this book more highly. Let these words change you.

STEPHAN BAUMAN

author of *Seeking Refugee* and former president/CEO of World Relief

For all who claim to be followers of Christ, this book is a timely "must read." To care for refugees is to touch the heart of God. God built the Hebrew nation out of a group of refugees. The incarnate Son was born into a refugee family. Repeatedly in the Scriptures God declares that the measure of a people is how we welcome aliens and refugees. Jesus himself says, "I was a stranger and you welcomed me." Given our era's unprecedented number of refugees and its rancorous debates, this book provides needed insights to shape our attitudes and actions.

TIM DEARBORN, PHD

former partnership leader for faith and development, World Vision International

Refugee Diaspora presents painful experiences of dislocated refugees in our time. The contributors, however, powerfully argue that the Lord's plan is to transform this people on the move to an army to witness to the God of salvation. The Holy Spirit loves to empower people from the margins, and the book signals another great season of harvest.

WONSUK MA, PHD

dean and professor of global Christianity, Oral Roberts University

Refugee Diaspora is a series of eye-opening, heart-wrenching, and soul-stirring narratives of the current global refugee crisis. It shows us what God and God's people are doing among the forcible displaced peoples of the world. It is a powerful call for all churches and Christians to get involved with the refugees across our streets and around the world. I encourage you to read it along with other church leaders.

ED STETZER, PHD, DMIN

Billy Graham Distinguished Chair of Church, Mission, and Evangelism,
Wheaton College

It is not enough for us to open our eyes. But it is a start. We need to listen and learn about the unique challenge and opportunity of refugees in our world today. We need to open our eyes, and then we need to open our hearts. These are people. These are individuals whose life is as precious as yours and mine. And we need to open our arms. It is not enough to learn or to empathize. I trust you will read this book and God will open your eyes, heart, and arms to the world that is on our doorstep. This is a unique gospel opportunity in our generation.

MICHAEL OH, PHD
Global CEO, The Lausanne Movement

This is a fascinating book unveiling how open hearts, open arms, open homes, and open churches can transform helpless refugees to become HOPE-FILLED followers of Jesus. This is a remarkable collection of global vignettes of how the Kingdom is expanding when human misery is met with God's mercy through the courage and compassion of God's people.

T. V. THOMAS, DMIN
chairman, Lausanne's Global Diaspora Network (GDN)

Carefully documented, insightful, arresting, compelling! *Refugee Diaspora* portrays one of the catastrophic global crises during the first quarter of the twenty-first century. This book is not all about disasters, agony, sufferings, injustice, and gloom! It is about compassion, mercy, justice, deliverance, and hope! All contributing writers are reflective practitioners calling everyone who knows God to stand up and take action.

SADIRI JOY TIRA, DMISS, DMIN
Catalyst for Diasporas, The Lausanne Movement

refugee diaspora

SAM GEORGE & MIRIAM ADENEY
EDITORS

refugee diaspora

Missions amid the Greatest
Humanitarian Crisis of our Times

Published by William Carey Publishing (formerly known as William Carey Library Publishers)
10 W. Dry Creek Cir | Littleton, CO 80120 | www.missionbooks.org

William Carey Publishing is a ministry of Frontier Ventures
1605 E. Elizabeth St | Pasadena, CA 91104 | www.frontierventures.org

Melissa Hicks, managing editor
Andrew Sloan, copyeditor
Kristopher K. Orr, cover design
Kristopher K. Orr and Mike Riester, interior design
Dr. Matthew Niermann and Jessica Rose of California Baptist University, infographics

Printed in the United States of America
22 21 20 19 18   1 2 3 4 5   BP1500

ISBN's: 978-0-87808-085-4 (paperback)
978-0-87808-086-1 (mobi)
978-0-87808-087-8 (epub)
LCCN: 2018043059

Library of Congress Cataloging-in-Publication Data

Names: George, Sam (Christian writer), editor. | Adeney, Miriam, 1945- editor.
Title: Refugee diaspora : missions amid the greatest humanitarian crisis of
   the world / Sam George and Miriam Adeney, editors.
Description: Littleton : William Carey Publishing, 2018. |
Identifiers: LCCN 2018043059 (print) | LCCN 2018044727 (ebook) | ISBN
   9780878080861 (mobi) | ISBN 9780878080878 (epub) | ISBN 9780878080854 (pbk.)
Subjects: LCSH: Church work with refugees. | Emigration and
   immigration--Religious aspects--Christianity. | Missions.
Classification: LCC BV4466 (ebook) | LCC BV4466 .R44 2018 (print) | DDC
   261.8/328--dc23
LC record available at https://lccn.loc.gov/2018043059

Acknowledgments

First of all, we are grateful to God who is moving powerfully among people who are forced to move from their homelands. Secondly, we are grateful to have met so many recent refugees who have become followers of Jesus—your transformation and passion to share Jesus is such an inspiration to all. Thirdly, we learned so much from hundreds who minister among refugees all over the world with such amazing devotion, selfless sacrifice, and limited resources. You are the real heroes of this book, though all could not be included in here.

The inspiration for this book struck me (Sam) while returning to Chicago from a refugee camp in Athens, Greece and within a few days, I was on my way to Panama City in Central America for a mission conference of the World Evangelical Alliance. There I ran into Dr. Miriam Adeney who had been a partner on various projects in the past and shared the idea for a book on global refugees. We sought advice from Dr. William Taylor and others who directed us to William Carey Publishing. Later, an article on refugees in the *Lausanne Global Analysis* titled "Is God Reviving Europe through Refugees"[1] received overwhelming response and many in the Lausanne family encouraged us to consider writing a book on refugees. Dr. Michael Oh, Dr. David Bennett, Dr. Joy Tira, and Dr. T.V. Thomas were instrumental in getting this project off the ground.

Special thanks are due to Denise Wynn of William Carey Publishing for all her guidance and all-out support for this project, while the publisher was going through a difficult transition. She and her team has done an exemplary work in copyediting, graphic design, layout, and marketing of this book, and they were a joy to work with. We express our gratitude to Dr. Matthew Niermann and Jessica Rose of the California Baptist University for all infographics in this book. We also express our sincere thanks to all endorsers for their kind words about this book.

We are also grateful to many who cheered us on for this project and labored quietly behind the scenes. Several friends stood with us in prayer and resources. Our families released us to travel to over two dozen countries. Some opened doors, hosted us, drove us around, introduced us to many refugee champions all over the world, and kept us safe in some dangerous places. Our sincere thanks.

Soli Deo Gloria
SAM GEORGE AND MIRIAM ADENEY
Summer 2018

1 Sam George, "Is God Reviving Europe through Refugees?" *Lausanne Global Analysis*, vol 6 (3), May 2017 https://www.lausanne.org/content/lga/2017-05/god-reviving-europe-refugees (accessed Jul 2018).

CONTENTS

**Section C: Reflections
(Biblical, Theological, and Missiological)**

LIST OF FIGURES AND TABLES

AUTHOR PROFILES

Sam George, PhD, serves as a global Catalyst for Diasporas of the Lausanne Movement. He is the author of several articles and books. He teaches World Christianity and Diaspora Missiology in many seminaries around the world. He holds degrees in Mechanical Engineering, Management, Theology, and Missiology. He lives with his family in the suburbs of Chicago (USA).

Miriam Adeney, PhD, is a cultural anthropologist and professor of World Christian Studies at Seattle Pacific University in Washington, USA. She teaches and speaks at universities and conferences regularly. She has written numerous articles and books on missions and trains Christian writers around the world.

Ken Kong serves as director of Southeast Asian Ministries for the Navigators. He is married to Rachel Kong. Both Rachel and Ken serve the Southeast Asian community in Long Beach, California, and are also serving in Southeast Asia.

Dr. Ahmad Karim (Afghanistan), pseudonym

Steven Rozzi is a Bay Area native who graduated from UC Berkeley with a BA in Sociology. His research interests include race, poverty and urban ethnography. He is passionate about facilitating informed public debate on social issues.

Russell Jeung, PhD, is chair and professor of Asian American Studies at San Francisco State University. He's the author of *At Home in Exile: Finding Jesus Among My Ancestors and Refugee Neighbors* (Zondervan, 2016) and the forthcoming book, *Family Sacrifices: The Worldviews and Ethics of Chinese Americans* (Oxford University Press, 2019).

J. Wu, PhD, Trinity Evangelical Divinity School, has served among Middle Eastern refugees since 2010. She is the author of *Mission Through Diaspora: The Case of the Chinese Church in the USA* (Langham Monographs, 2016). She and her husband currently live and serve in the Middle East.

Peter M. Sensenig, PhD, is a regional interfaith consultant for the Mennonite Board in East Africa. He has taught in Somaliland, Djibouti, and the United States, and currently resides in Zanzibar, Tanzania. He holds a PhD in Theology and Christian Ethics from Fuller Theological Seminary. He has published on just peacemaking, Christian ethics, and peacemaking leadership.

DR. WISSAM PAULUS KAMMOU is an associate pastor of a Christian and Missionary Alliance Church in Iraq. He is also a practicing dentist. Born and raised in Baghdad as a Catholic, Wissam came to receive Christ in his university days. He and his wife and two children moved to the province of Erbil in northern Iraq.

KEVIN PANICKER served in East Africa with the international relief division of Samaritan's Purse. He earned a bachelor's degree in International Studies at the University of Richmond and a master's degree at Fuller Theological Seminary. Indian by heritage, Kenyan by birth, American by citizenship, and a global missionary, Kevin currently lives in Manila, Philippines.

JOSÉ RM PRADO is the founder & CEO of Dignità and Brazilian facilitator of the Refugee Highway Partnership. Dignità is a humanitarian NGO that affirms and defends human dignity, justice, and a culture of peace. He serves as a catalyst for cooperation and collaboration among global ministries serving with and for refugees and forcibly displaced peoples.

TORLI KRUA fled war-torn Liberia for Boston in 1990 and now serves as a human rights activist and missionary to refugee communities and African immigrants in the New England area. He serves as director of the Greater Boston Refugee Ministry of the Emmanuel Gospel Center in Boston.

MARTIN WIGHTMAN is a Canadian journalist based in New Brunswick. He leads a nonprofit organization that provides affordable urban housing and has volunteered to help welcome and resettle former refugees and other newcomers to Canada. He writes about science, geography, and religion.

PETEER VIMALASEKARAN, DMIN has lived and worked among refugees in Europe since 1998. He fled Sri Lanka during civil war and studied theology in UK and USA. He serves as director of refugee ministries of European Christian Mission and lives with his family in Karlsruhe, Germany.

DANIEL ZEIDAN serves as a ministry strategist for Samaritan's Purse. Earlier he served an international NGO, supervising projects in Latin America and Africa, and a UK-based mission agency. He holds master's degrees in development and theology from Cambridge and Edinburgh Universities. Daniel and his wife, Barbara, and their two sons live in La Paz, Bolivia.

JULIA KAPUKI JADA is a graduate of the University of Juba in Sociology and Social Anthropology and earned a master's degree in Social Change from Istanbul University. She is also a graduate of River Bible Institute in Turkey. Formerly, served with International Fellowship of Evangelical Students in Sudan and currently serves as a lecturer at the University of Juba.

DR. CAMILLE MELKI is the founder and executive director of Heart for Lebanon based in Beirut. Along with providing humanitarian aid to redeem the dignity and address the needs of refugees, Heart for Lebanon empowers local communities to overcome poverty, dependency, injustice, and marginalization and to holistically transform lives of at-risk children.

STEPHEN CARTER serves with Middle East Concern, an association of Christian agencies and individuals that support those in the Middle East and North Africa who are marginalized, discriminated against, or persecuted for being or becoming Christians. He has lived nearly half his life in the Middle East region. Stephen holds a BA in Biblical and Intercultural Studies (Open University, UK) and an MA in Social and Political Sciences (Cambridge University), and he has extensive experience in human rights, public policy, and the rule of law.

SAJI OOMMEN was born to Asian Indian parents in Dallas, Texas. He earned an MBA in Global Economic Development from Eastern University and has spent the last fifteen years in India, Canada, and Turkey. A social entrepreneur, Saji has started a bakery and a travel company and is currently pursuing his passion for peace through Building Leaders 4 Peace (BL4P).

TABITHA MCDUFFEE is the founder of FaithandForcedMigration.com, an online resource for Christians serving refugees. She holds a BA in Biblical and Intercultural Studies from Moody Bible Institute and is pursuing an MA in Refugee Law and Forced Migration from the University of London. Tabitha serves with World Relief and lives with her husband in the suburbs of Chicago.

CHRIS WRIGHT, PHD, Cambridge, is an Anglican clergyman and an Old Testament scholar. He is currently the international ministries director of Langham Partnership International. He was the principal of All Nations Christian College. He is an honorary member of All Souls Church, Langham Place, in London, UK and author of many scholarly publications.

PAUL SYDNOR, PHD, serves as the European leader for the International Association for Refugees. He is a Presbyterian pastor and a cofounder of the Refugee Highway Partnership (RHP) in Europe. Paul holds an MDiv and MA in counseling from Gordon-Conwell and a PhD from the Oxford Centre for Mission Studies. He lives in Lille, France.

YOUSEF KAMAL ALKHOURI is a Christian Arab Palestinian. He received a bachelor's degree in Biblical Studies and Christian Education from Bethlehem Bible College in Bethlehem, Palestine, and recently completed the Master of Divinity program at the Alliance Theological Seminary, New York. He now lives in Bethlehem, Palestine and teaches Bible and theology at Bethlehem Bible College.

Introduction

SAM GEORGE, PHD

Soon after our family's Thanksgiving meal in Chicago in 2016, I flew to Germany on a ministry trip that I called "Jesus Was A Refugee." The plan was to travel through several cities in Europe that were hosting refugees from the war zones of the Middle East and elsewhere in order to learn what God was doing among them and to share about the fact that Jesus was also a refugee. Many of those refugees were spending their first Christmas in a Western nation, and I wanted to retell the Christmas story in a manner that they could relate to. They had endured insurmountable odds in recent months and were glad to be alive. My interactions with refugees in Europe in the days prior to Christmas infused a deeper meaning to my Christmas season and a new vision of how Christians could serve refugees everywhere.

When I arrived in Germany I was taken to a retreat center where a local refugee ministry team had organized a meeting for the recently arrived refugees in and around Bremen, Germany. We were joined by worship leaders and evangelists from Egypt and the United States. Nearly one hundred refugees from Syrian, Kurdish, Yazidi, Iraqi, Druze, Sudanese, and Somali backgrounds had come together for a weekend Christian conference, the first one ever for most of them. The Arabic music and fellowship times were deeply moving and profound. I heard many soul-stirring testimonies from refugees and sensed a deep-seated yearning for God among them. They asked the conference leaders many questions, which were answered lovingly and patiently, late into night. On the last evening of the conference, it was touching to witness the overwhelming response of the refugees to the gospel call as they surrendered their lives to Jesus.

In the subsequent three weeks I participated in several special events organized for refugees in different cities of Germany and other countries of Western Europe. I witnessed enormous eagerness among refugees toward Jesus and enthusiastic response to the gospel. Many of them had dreams and visions of *Isa* or shared about miraculous encounters with Jesus. Their passion and their newfound faith allegiance were remarkable and awe-inspiring. I had the opportunity to visit several refugee camps and to meet Christian leaders, businessmen, policemen, and policymakers in several countries. I sat with them, ate with them, talked with them, sang with them, played with them, and listened to their stories. What a unique and unforgettable Christmas season!

In the birth narrative of Jesus in the Gospel of Matthew, we read that Jesus was a refugee too. After the popular story of the visit of the wise men who brought gifts to baby Jesus, we find tucked in just three verses (2:13–15) an incident that seldom gets noticed during Christmastime. When the wise men didn't return to Jerusalem, as instructed by King Herod, to report the whereabouts of the newborn king of the Jews—whom the king of Judea perceived as a potential threat to his own throne—Herod ordered the mass murder of all baby boys under the age of two in the town of Bethlehem. However, before the edict was implemented, the earthly father of Jesus, Joseph the carpenter from Nazareth, was warned in a dream of the ensuing threat to the child's life and was told to take Jesus and his mother and flee to Egypt. In the cover of night, Joseph escaped before King Herod's soldiers came and executed all the baby boys in Bethlehem. Joseph, Mary, and Jesus stayed in Egypt until Herod died and Joseph was instructed by an angel to return to Nazareth.

The Egyptian and North African Christians still recount the tale of baby Jesus coming to their land as a refugee. They recite poetically, "When the Son of God was born into the world, when king was hunting to destroy the baby, an angel told his parents to escape to a neighboring country, and the Savior of the World found shelter in our land." Egyptians continue to proudly retell the openness and kindness of their forefathers to foreigners when their lives were in danger. They gratefully reminisce how a simple act of hospitality to strangers was a blessing to their land and people for many generations and centuries, even to the present time. Quite interestingly, I found numerous Christians of Egyptian descent in Europe who are still involved in ministries of welcoming and serving refugees arriving there!

Over the last three months of 2016 and over many trips in 2017, I was present at meetings where hundreds of refugees turned to Christ, and I visited several Christian fellowship groups and churches where hundreds of refugees have been baptized. One church in Germany had baptized over a thousand Syrian and Kurdish believers during the last six months of 2016. At our meetings each night in different cities in Sweden, Denmark, Austria, Greece, Germany, and Switzerland, I witnessed hundreds of refugees receiving Jesus as Lord of their lives. The Middle Eastern Christians in Europe are not only very engaged with the crisis but also highly effective on account of their linguistic and cultural proximity to the refugees. I only wish more European churches would take notice of the Middle Eastern Christians God has already brought into their midst well before the current refugee crisis erupted in that part of the world and elsewhere.

I believe that one of the ways God is reviving Christianity in Europe is through refugees. They may be the least likely agents for a major move of God. But isn't that what the Christmas story is all about? A teenage girl, a carpenter, a manger, shepherds, Persian astrologers, Bethlehem, and the like. God breaks into our world where we least expect it. A set of very unlikely agents in unsuspected circumstances orchestrating God's story of salvation—all precisely occurring as foretold centuries prior. That is God's way of entering into the world and changing the world. The refugees are God-bearers (*theotokos*) reviving the stagnant churches in Europe and being used by God in the same way that God has always operated through people who are willing to risk all to bring him into our world.

REFUGEE SITUATION: THE GREATEST HUMANITARIAN CRISIS OF OUR TIMES

Who can forget Aylan Kurdi, the three-year-old Syrian boy of Kurdish background whose dead body was washed up on the shores of Turkey? Who will ever know the countless men, women, and children who drowned in the depths of the Mediterranean Sea or were buried in the deserts of Syria or Iraq? How could anyone assess the incalculable abuse and trauma refugees have suffered at the hands of violent gangs and border security forces as they sought shelter? Or the enormous amount of wealth created by human traffickers as a result of human displacement unprecedented in history? What are some of the immediate and long-term repercussions of policy changes toward refugees and foreigners in many nations?

As I traveled across many countries in Europe, I often heard from people and read news reports about the dire situation of the growing refugee problem. I met a young man who miraculously escaped the clutches of a radical extremist group in Iraq and a Syrian teenage girl who was repeatedly raped by terrorists and sold to traffickers. Unable to recount the details of the brutality they suffered, several made indirect references to family members who were killed. I was deeply moved by the myriad of heart-wrenching stories of escape, loss, survival, endurance, and hope in the midst of the most extreme circumstances one could ever encounter in life.

I also heard firsthand from native European host families, pastors, storekeepers, students, business leaders, and politicians about the widespread fear and anxiety concerning refugees. Some people are petrified by the prospect of the end of prosperity, security, familiarity, and their normal way of life. They believe that migrants should be kept away in order to preserve jobs and health and welfare services. The potential of government austerity measures, social instability, and the rise in unemployment on account of the flight of jobs to faraway places is producing a cold-heartedness stemming from a deep sense of trepidation and insecurity. Some are gripped by the fear of potential harm that refugees could unleash on them and the ever-present danger of terrorist activities. The media coverage has only fanned the flames of terror among native Europeans.

The current refugee situation is sometimes referred to as "the greatest humanitarian crisis of our times." That might be true in a sense, since such a dispersal of humanity has not occurred since the Second World War. However, that is only part of the worldwide refugee crisis, and countless more refugees have been languishing in others parts of the world for years but did not receive any media attention or support from humanitarian agencies. Many are no longer with us to tell the harrowing stories of what they have undergone as a result of their forceful displacement from their homeland.

Seeking to find what God is doing in the midst of this crisis, this volume contains stories about refugees fleeing conflicts in Cambodia, Sri Lanka, Afghanistan, Iraq, and Syria, as well as stories from the nations where they are arriving—like the US, Canada, the UK, Brazil, and Germany. It narrates people being forcefully displaced on account of geopolitical upheavals, such as in Sudan, Turkey, and Myanmar, along with natural calamities like that in Somalia. The nations that have welcomed "your tired, your poor, your huddled masses yearning to breathe free" and "the wretched refuse of your teeming shore"[1] have received special favor from God, who watches over the poor and marginalized not only to ignite faith in refugees but also to inject new life into the Christianity of the host nations.

The contemporary refugee crisis seems to have stirred our collective consciousness and changed the course of many nations, and our world, permanently. The current forceful human displacement has catapulted immigration into major sociocultural and legal deliberations. It has come to the forefront of security and electoral agendas in several countries. It has

---

1 Words from the plaque on the base of the Statue of Liberty in New York. From the poem "The New Colossus," written by American poet Emma Lazarus in 1883.

redefined developmental and economic agendas in many parts of the world. These disruptions have already reshaped our world in many significant ways and will continue to reshape our future, far beyond our current imaginations.

REFUGEE OPPORTUNITY: THE GREAT POTENTIAL

The Chinese word for crisis is said to be composed of two characters—one represents danger and the other represents opportunity. Every crisis often comes with new possibilities, and a crisis can be an opportunity when seen through the eyes of faith and handled correctly by the right people. This could be true of the current refugee crisis. God seems to be using this crisis to do something new—not only in Europe, where some of the refugees have arrived, but also in cracking open the Middle East for the gospel in new ways.

The reaction of Christians to the refugee crisis generally vacillates between fear and compassion. Most Christians are indifferent or apathetic, often unable to fathom the desperation of these people since they have never been exposed to the harsh realities of war like the regions of the world where conflicts are regular features. When Christians in the West see the plight of the refugees fleeing Iraq and Syria, some react against their own governments who have created the conflicts which led to the refugee problems, while others attribute the crisis to the refugee nations' own making. Some are eager to extend a helping hand in the form of food and blankets, while many feel helpless in light of the refugee influx. No matter what they do or how much they help, there seems to be no end of incoming refugees.

Some churches and Christians in Europe have established refugee welcome or assistance centers—ranging from handing out welcome packs to providing language training or employment. A sizable number of refugees have responded to the gospel of Jesus Christ in many cities of Europe and elsewhere; and many church and ministry leaders have reported remarkable outcomes for their efforts in engaging Syrian and Kurdish refugees, in particular, who arrived in their cities in the past year or so. Many vehemently reject the faith they were raised in and what people have done to their homeland in the name of religion.

Numerous Bible study groups and fellowship groups have been started in various cities. Other refugees passionately argue about faith matters and try to make sense of their lives and forced displacement. Several new churches have been birthed on account of new refugee Christians; and the Alliance of Arabic Churches in Europe, comprised of some two hundred churches, has been created. There are also churches affiliated with other denominations and networks that have not have joined the alliance. A conservative estimate is that there are twice as many as churches that are independent or part of other associations. Most of these fellowship groups and churches are under-resourced and led by lay or bi-vocational ministers. They utilize their cultural affinity, personal Christian experience, and minimal knowledge of Scripture to minister to refugees. Some draw from their Christian upbringing in the Middle East while other utilize resources from Christian ministries to Muslims to a great extent.

Since nearly all refugees come from a highly religious culture, there is no need to prove the existence of God or to start your apologetic that there is one true God. The irony is that in the face of a post-Christian, agnostic/atheistic worldview in Western Europe, the spiritual and religious fervor of the refugees is reigniting a spiritual quest on the part of Europeans for their own heritage. Most refugees come from predominantly Islamic nations with strong convictions about God and sinful behaviors. Most have been exposed to Jesus as a prophet and hold a high view of *Nabi Isa*—surprisingly, higher than that of some Europeans! These refugees are shocked that many citizens of their host countries don't believe in God or aren't involved in churches, and therefore become ardent evangelists in the course of their refugee wanderings.

What seems very astonishing, however, is that many refugees have seen dreams or visions or heard supernatural utterances from God.[2] Some have had divine encounters and others have received physical healing in their bodies or experienced miracles of some sort. Their mere survival at such exceptional odds is a miracle in itself. Their yearning for spiritual things and a divine being arise out of their deep anguish of experiences, as they wonder why they have survived while so many of their friends or family did not. As nations and global agencies try to figure out policies and resources to handle the unprecedented influx of refugees from war-torn Syria and Iraq to Europe, God seems to be actively involved in drawing many refugees to himself and using them to revive faith in Europe. Who could have thought of such a brilliant strategy? It is akin to hitting two birds with one stone.

Religious persecution and refugee movements have been strategic inflection points in the history of Christianity, and current refugee displacements will reshape the future of Christianity in many ways. In the apostolic era, some of the refugees who fled from the persecution in Jerusalem were welcomed by the believers in Antioch (Acts 8:1; 11:19–21), and the conversion of Paul (Acts 9) resulted in a dramatic transformation of the persecutor. Later, in AD 313, the Roman emperor Constantine issued the Edict of Milan, which

---

2 These experiences are consistent with appearances of Jesus among Islamic communities globally, as recorded by David Garrison in *A Wind in the House of Islam: How God Is Drawing Muslims around the World to Faith in Jesus Christ* (Monument, CO: Wigtake Resources, 2014).

ended empire-wide persecution of Christians, and a doctrinal crisis arose over the deity of Jesus Christ, resulting in the persecution of various groups until the church council at Nicaea in 325. The Great Schism of 1054, which divided the church between the East and the West, also resulted in religious mistreatment of many sects of believers. And the Protestant Reformation of the sixteenth century created religious refugees all over Europe. The Pilgrims who sailed across the Atlantic to the New World on the Mayflower in 1620 were seeking religious freedom and escaping persecution in their home country. Today Christians around the world continue to show exceptional generosity and hospitality to those who are fleeing for their lives, as you will see in the ensuing chapters of this book.

DIASPORA MISSIOLOGY: REFUGEE DIMENSIONS

According to Andrew Walls, the center of Christianity is always on the move; the center of gravity of Christianity has shifted, and margins continually revitalize the center.[3] This is evident from the recent demographic shift of Christianity from the Global North to the Global South.[4] Mission theology is a continual work in progress, moving toward greater inclusivity. Mission in the margins always emerges in unclear forms, but it is characterized by clear signs of advancement of the gospel, empowerment by the Holy Spirit, and—as a result—changes to the very nature of Christian faith and our conceptions of it. Therefore, Christian mission is a boundary-breaking phenomenon, diffusing across cultures and geographies relentlessly, and human displacement has always played a vital role in reshaping Christianity.

God is sovereign over human dispersion, whether it be willful or forced and regardless of the motives, routes, or conditions. All forms of human displacement create complex crises in life, relationships, and beliefs. Migration is fundamentally a "theologizing experience," [5] and displaced people are forced to question underlying assumptions about existence, people, identity, origin, purpose, meaning, worldviews, and ultimately God. They are open to explore new ideas and reject old ways of life. Their past beliefs and practices are less binding, even as they are forced to reconsider family and community in the new world. When exposed to new contexts, displaced people begin to assimilate to dominant cultures; and comparisons are constantly made between the world they left behind and the new world before them. By interpreting both worlds

---

3 Andrew F. Walls, *The Cross-Cultural Process in Christian History* (New York: Orbis Books, 2002), 31.

4 Several works attest to this trend, such as Philip Jenkins, *The Next Christendom* (2011); Samuel Escobar, *The New Global Mission* (2003); David Barrett, *World Christian Encyclopedia* (2001); Todd Johnson and Kenneth Ross, *Atlas of Global Christianity* (2009); and Lamin Sanneh, *Whose Religion Is Christianity?* (2003).

5 Timothy Smith, "Religion and Ethnicity in America," in *The American Historical Review* 83 (5): 1175.

to each other, they become adept at translations and facilitate cultural diffusion of life and faith matters as well. They counteract the challenges of uprooting, transplantation, and survival in a new world by turning to spiritual realities and to others with a spiritual outlook.

In our contemporary world, people are on the move everywhere at unprecedented levels.[6] God is also on the move among people on the move, as evident from the fact that many refugees are turning to Christ and becoming a means to revive Christianity in Europe and elsewhere. The diasporas arising out of forced displacement, including the current flight of refugees, are fertile ground for new divine activity and with it the advancement and transformation of Christianity. In Christian history, persecution has always been a strategic inflection point and played a critical role in its decline as well as expansion.[7]

God seems to be doing many new things in and through today's refugees worldwide, just as he did through other forms of migration throughout human history. Most displaced people in the world tend to be Christians or embrace Christianity after migrating to foreign countries. The diasporic communities have played a strategic role in the creation and advancement of Christianity from its very inception. Just as the Jewish diaspora of the first century helped Christians to scatter and resulted in the diffusion of Christianity to the Gentiles, today's diasporas—including refugees—are renewing and advancing Christianity in unanticipated ways. Diaspora missiology[8] has emerged as a major thrust for the global church in the twenty-first century, and all forms of displaced people are on the forefront of the renewal of Christianity itself.

In the first century, the Jewish diaspora and religious persecution forced the small Jewish sect of Jesus' followers to be widely scattered. The disciples of Jesus were commanded to go to the ends of earth (Matt 28:19) and to be witnesses of Jesus in Jerusalem, Judea, Samaria, and the ends of the earth (Acts 1:8). After Jesus' ascension, however, his disciples did not depart from Jerusalem, as instructed by their master in order to receive the promised Holy Spirit and fear of the Jewish leaders and the Roman authorities. As the early church grew, it came under severe persecution, and the believers were forced to scatter to places far and wide. The dispersed believers reached out to fellow Jews as well as Gentiles, causing the faith to transcend the ethnic and cultural boundaries of the Christian faith. The scattered Jews were quick to embrace and proclaim the Christian message in their adopted homelands all over the Mediterranean world.

---

6 For more on how global migration is reshaping our world, see Ian Goldin et al., *Exceptional People* (2011); W. M. Spellman, *The Global Community* (2002); and Robin Cohen, *Global Diaspora* (2008).

7 See Jehu Hanciles, *Beyond Christendom* (2012), and Andrew Walls, *The Missionary Movement in Christian History* (1995).

8 For more on diaspora missiology, see Sadiri Joy and Tetsunao Yamamori, *Scattered and Gathered* (2016); Enoch Wan, *Diaspora Missiology* (2011); and Chandler Im and Amos Yong, *Global Diasporas and Missions* (2015).

In the year of the five hundredth anniversary of the Protestant Reformation, God is once again reviving the church in Europe, this time through refugees from the Middle East. Who could have foreseen something like this? The churches and ministries who are involved in welcoming refugees or ministering to them are experiencing renewal, while those who are skeptical about them are missing out on a move of the Spirit. God is indeed doing new things in the world. What a privilege it is to see him at work where you least expect it!

Andrew Walls is right in his claim that "Migration is a more significant factor in Christian history than the Reformation itself."[9] What was said about the great European migration and spread of Christianity from its heartland in the sixteenth and seventeenth centuries to other continents could now be extended to the reversal of human flow (including the current refugee movement) from Africa, the Middle East, Asia, and elsewhere to Europe. In the course of discussing "reverse mission" and chronicling the impact of African Christians on Europe at the beginning of the twenty-first century, an African diaspora scholar described Europe as a "prodigal continent."[10] Now that role is also being taken up by new Christians of Middle Eastern descent and Asians who are bringing a new lease of life to a moribund and plateaued European Christianity. Just as the great European migration took the Christian faith to the far ends of the world, now Christians from those same margins are returning the favor by bringing a fresh vitality to churches in Europe.

CONFUSION OVER MULTIPLE TERMS: DEFINITIONS

Who are refugees, really? A brief survey of terms will help us address precisely who we are talking about. People, both in scholarly circles and casual conversations, use a variety of terms to describe refugees without really knowing the various nuances of their meaning, which often adds to the confusion over this issue. Some tend to use the terms interchangeably, without making any clear distinctions between them. These terms[11] include *aliens, asylum seekers, diaspora, displaced people, ethnic minority, expatriate, foreigners, forced or involuntary migrants, illegals, immigrants, refugees, stateless, trafficked, undocumented,* and *uprooted people.*

---

9 Andrew Walls, "The Great Commission 1910–2010" A lecture delivered at the University of Edinburgh in 2003 and unpublished paper.

10 Afe Adogame, *The African Christian Diaspora: New Currents and Emerging Trends in World Christianity* (London: Bloomsbury, 2013), 169.

11 For a detailed definition of various associated terms, see the glossary in Mark Gibney, *Global Refugee Crisis,* 2nd ed., 2010; and the glossary by Tereso Casino and Charles Cook, in Sadiri Joy Tira and Tetsunao Yamamori, *Scattered and Gathered: A Global Compendium on Diaspora Missiology,* 2016.

DEFINITION OF TERMS

Alien is commonly used to refer to any individual who is not a national of the state in which he or she is present.

Asylum refers to the protection given by one country to people from another country when their lives come under serious threat. Refugees may be temporarily granted asylum in one country before they are transferred or resettled more permanently in another country.

Asylum seeker is a person who has fled from his or her home country and is seeking refugee status in another country.

Displaced people are those who either choose to or are forced to relocate to another part of the country (known as internal or domestic migration) or another country (international migration). The displacement may either be temporary or more permanent, in which case the focus is on geographical relocation. When the individual chooses of his own free to relocate to another place, it is considered voluntary migration. However, when displacement is coerced or forced upon the individual due to natural calamities, conflicts, political instability, or subjugation, it is referred to as involuntary migration.

Forced migration involves the movement of people on account of some form of coercion, including threats to life and livelihood, arising out of natural or manmade causes.

Foreign born people are those who are born in a country other than where they now reside. They may have become naturalized citizen of the receiving nation or have citizenship elsewhere while maintaining valid permit to live and work in another country.

Human trafficking involves the forceful exploitation of people by taking them away from their family, community, and places of familiarity for monetary gains for purposes such as prostitution, sexual abuse, slavery, organ harvesting, etc.

Illegal migrants are people who entered another country without valid visa or identity.

Immigrant is an all-encompassing term referring to someone who leaves their native land and goes to live in another country for either a given period or permanently. It does not include tourists or vacationers.

Internally displaced people (IDP) have been forcefully displaced from their places or birth and/or residence by natural or environmental disasters, chemical or nuclear disasters, or famine or development projects to other places within their own country. They do not cross national borders.

Stateless persons have been denied national identity documents or have had them removed.

Undocumented individuals don't meet a host country's legal conditions for immigration. Sometimes they are called illegal aliens or simply "illegals."

Uprooted people are those who have left family and the culture of their birth or upbringing to live in another place and culture. This encompasses all forms of migrants, including refugees.

Diaspora is a Greek biblical word, meaning "scattered" or "dispersion." This term was originally used in the context of the Jewish dispersion and life in exile, but it has been increasingly used to refer to all forms of displaced people, including refugees. The reason for their relocation from the land of their birth varies widely, as well as the situation of their border crossing. In Christian mission circles, diaspora is a missional means decreed and blessed by God (Gen 1:28; 9:1; 12:3; 28:14), under his sovereign rule, to promote the expansion of his kingdom and the fulfilment of the Great Commission (Matt 24:14; 28:18–20).

Refugees are people who have been uprooted from their homes and forced to seek shelter in a foreign country. They flee their homelands and look for a place where they can find protection and provisions for life. According to the UN Refugee Agency, "A refugee has a well-founded fear of persecution for reasons of race, religion, nationality, political opinion or membership in a particular social group. Most likely, they cannot return home or are afraid to do so."[12] Our focus in this book is on refugees who are forced to flee their homelands because of war and other extreme circumstances. This does not include internally displaced people or other types of displaced people—not that they are unimportant or unworthy of investigation. Moreover, we limit our scope to major conflict regions of the world, roughly in the last five decades. We highlight refugee movements arising from major geopolitical conflicts during that period, identifying people who could tell their stories with distinct thrust. Most of these individuals share a contemporary assessment of that particular refugee situation from their own vantage point and write from a Christian missionary perspective.

---

12 "What Is a Refugee?" The UN Refugee Agency website, http://www.unrefugees.org/what-is-a-refugee/ (accessed August 2, 2018).

REFUGEES OF THE WORLD: A GLOBAL PERSPECTIVE

While the recent refugee influx into Europe has received pervasive coverage by the Western media, we don't hear much about the millions of refugees hosted in other countries of the world. In fact, nearly 85 percent of the world refugee population are in the non-Western world. Even as Western nations anguish over a few thousand refugee settlement applicants, neighboring nations in conflict regions bear the greatest brunt of the refugee crises. The geographical proximity alone determines the humanitarian obligation—as in the case of Lebanon, where over two million Syrians have fled from civil war, or Kenya, which has absorbed over a million people driven across its borders by drought, famine, and regional conflicts.

Figure 1: Forcibly Displaced People of the World (Source—UNHCR/2018)

68.5 million forcibly displaced people worldwide

Internally Displaced People
40 million

Refugees
25.4 million
19.9 million under UNHCR mandate
5.4 million Palestinian refugees registered by UNRWA

Asylum-seekers
3.1 million

According to the latest data from the United Nations, in the middle of 2018 there were over sixty-eight million forcibly displaced people in the world and of which over twenty-five million are categorized as refugees. Countless numbers of them, no doubt, are no longer alive to tell their stories. Below you will see a chart of the world refugee population since 1970, along with maps highlighting both refugee-sending and refugee-receiving nations. Historically refugees have ended up in neighboring countries; only in recent years have we seen refugees crossing through many nations to reach countries farther away. Still, only a very few make it to Western industrialized nations. The overwhelming majority are given shelter in refugee camps in neighboring countries—for years and even decades in many cases.

As of January 2017, the sprawling tent city of Dadaab in northeastern Kenya hosted over 350,000 refugees, mostly from neighboring Somalia, making it the largest refugee camp in the world. Over 100,000 made a perilous journey from Yemen to the Horn of Africa in Djibouti and Ethiopia. Some 5,000 refugees drowned in 2016 trying to cross the Mediterranean Sea from Libya to Italy.

Because of the war in Syria, thousands of refugees arrived every day on the Greek island of Lesbos after crossing the Aegean Sea from Turkey. There are nearly three million Afghan refugees in Pakistan. A few hundred thousand Biharis of India who call themselves Pakistanis to live in refugee camps in Bangladesh, even as thousands of Bangaldeshis live in Kolkota and Assam regions of India as refugees. Thousands of Rohingya refugees shuttle between Bangladesh and Myanmar. A spike in violence in the Central American nations of El Salvador, Honduras, and Guatemala in 2015 caused a surge in unaccompanied minors journeying northward, seeking asylum in the United States.

Over half the world's refugees are children, some being born in refugee camps and never even seeing the world outside of the camp. Women and small children are the most vulnerable in the perilous crossings. It is estimated that refugees remain displaced for an average of eighteen years. Educational and vocational opportunities are scarce, and health care needs are severely overlooked. Refugee camps are often overcrowded, accommodating more than their intended capacity. Makeshift housing in abandoned buildings without running water, sewage, or electricity is common. The plight of these refuges who wait indefinitely for someone to accept their asylum plea is incomprehensible.

Many forcefully displaced people never make it to their desired destination. They remain trapped in refugee camps for decades or fall by the wayside along the treacherous travels. Many are abused by security forces, and some are killed by traffickers. Many suffer common diseases without timely medical help, while many others are cheated of their life savings. Many bear the marks of abuse and gun wounds for the rest of their lives. Millions of minors are sold into child labor and sexual slavery. Some estimate that the human trafficking business has flourished manifold on account of the current refugee crisis. The crisis has also exposed governmental and institutional lethargy, the obsolescence of policies, the emotional impulse of the masses, and politicians who are quick to take advantage of the situation to frame new laws or gain power. Due to the looming shortage of funds and the absence of protective measures for the victims of wars, many are ending up in need of compassion, aid, and refuge from the rest of the world.

Never before in human history have we been so inundated with reports and images of atrocities happening across the globe. In an age of unprecedented mass displacement, the world needs an unprecedented humanitarian response and a renewed global commitment to protect people fleeing conflict and persecution. To sustain our sympathies, we seem to be relying solely on short-term dosages of compassion homilies and the daily news headlines. The problem is, these injections come in diverse forms and are not sustainable over time. Sometimes they reawaken genuine compassion, but in most occasions they simply reinforce the existing fear and instinct for self-protection.

BOOK OUTLINE

This volume is divided into three broad sections: Regions, Responses, and Reflections. The Regions section contains nine chapters that provide snapshots of refugee situations in different parts of the world, including two autobiographical narratives of refugee displacement out of Cambodia and Afghanistan. Other accounts include refugee situations in Africa, Syrians in Jordan, Karen Burmese in Oakland (California), and other stories told from Afghanistan, Iraq, Liberia, Somalia, and Brazil.

The Responses section, comprised of nine more chapters which presents compelling case studies of refugee ministries in the form of advocacy, counseling, justice, peacemaking and solidarity. They come from Canada, Germany, Greece, South Sudan, Lebanon, the UK, Turkey, and the US and are written by people from diverse professional backgrounds, such as activists, bloggers, educators, evangelists, missionaries, pastors, psychologists, and social workers. Throughout this section you will find many interesting facts and the latest data, as well as maps of refugee populations of the world.

The Reflections section, comprised of three chapters of biblical, theological, and missiological reflections, expounds the scriptural directive to care for those who have been forced to flee and God's heart for those in the margins of our world. It attempts to develop a theology of migration and a theology of the church in light of the current refugee crisis written from locations such as London, Paris and Bethlehem. Finally, Miriam Adeney closes with some pertinent highlights emerging out of this volume, along with the mission challenge before the global church in the face of the greatest humanitarian crisis of our times.

BETHLEHEM OR EGYPT:
NO ROOM IN THE INN, OR WELCOMING

The two common responses of the global church in the face of the refugee crisis can be metaphorically depicted by two places in the Christmas story: Bethlehem and Egypt—more precisely, the people of those places and how they responded differently in the birth narrative of Jesus. The former place did not offer lodging, while the latter offered shelter to the young family who was escaping the edict of extermination. The angelic intervention directs an unexpected journey for the holy family in order to thwart the schemes of a political psychopath.

When Emperor Caesar Augustus decreed a census, Jesus' parents were forced to make the treacherous journey from Galilee to Bethlehem—their destination being the famous birthplace of David, the great king of Israel. Bethlehem, however, paled in comparison to Jerusalem, the capital David established and the center of the political power of Herod the Great. Since the remote village of David's birthplace did not have sufficient housing options when the pregnant couple arrived in their ancestral homeland for the official census, they were informed that there was "no room in the inn" (Luke 2:7). Mary gave birth to Jesus in that isolated village and wrapped the newborn in cloths and laid him in a manger. While still in the womb, Jesus experienced rejection as there was no room for him in the world, and it took incredible courage for Mary and Joseph to believe God's message and bring Jesus into the world. Likewise, many refugees are showing extraordinary courage and faith by risking their very lives to bring Jesus afresh into their lives and our world.

In the face of great danger, an angel instructed the new parents to take the baby and escape to Egypt. Although the biblical account doesn't provide details about where they went in Egypt and how they were treated there, it is safe to assume they lived comfortably for some time until an angel instructed Joseph to make a return voyage all the way back to Nazareth. The people of Egypt extended welcome and cared for this family who was on the run for their lives. They might have offered housing and provisions for the family.

Our response to the plight of current refugees is no different. We either have no room for them in our crowded cities and slumping economies or we try to create room in our hearts and neighborhoods in spite of practical inconveniences and cultural differences. Either we are moved by genuine compassion or we are filled with inextricable fear regarding how these recently arrived refugees will disrupt our way of life. If only we realized how others created room for us (or our ancestors) when we first arrived, we would be more considerate of our fellow human beings who have suffered much for no mistake of their own. If only we could see the image of God in the face of refugees, even if they have a different skin color or speak a different language. If only we believed in the biblical commands to care for the poor, the orphans, and the aliens, even when it pinches our pockets and creates momentary discomfort. If only we realized that God wants to meet us through refugees and that in exchange for the material blessings we offer to refugees, they will offer spiritual blessings to us and our nations in return. Refugees address the desperate needs that we don't even realize we have.

SECTION A:

Regions

(Asia, Middle East, Africa, Europe, and Americas)

chapter one

From Genocide to Kingdom–building in Cambodia

KEN KONG

BORN TO RUN: OUT OF CAMBODIA

My parents were in their teens when they first met in the Pursat labor camp in Cambodia. Their meeting wasn't something they planned themselves. It was arranged by the Khmer Rouge. They went to my father and said, "Mut (comrade), you see that woman? That is the woman we want you to marry."

My father responded, "Can I meet with this woman in person?"

Then the Khmer Rouge went to my mother and said, "Mut, you see that man? That is the man we want you to marry. If you don't agree to this we will execute both you and that man."

Due to my father's request, they arranged the first meeting between my mom and dad. After that brief encounter, my dad left feeling and knowing that he was in love with my mom.

Their wedding was simple and with no fanfare. The Khmer Rouge wrapped a dirty old scarf around their hands and gave the pronouncement that they were married. This was the beginning of a journey between my father and mother. I was born in the winter of 1978 during the reign of Pol Pot and the Khmer Rouge government, which lasted from 1975 until 1979. My mother gave birth to me in the Pursat labor camp, where she worked day and night. At that time, my father was stationed in the Siem Reap labor camp (a three-to-four-day walk from Pursat). In that camp they were forced to dig and gather rocks for no apparent purpose other than to do what the Khmer Rouge wanted them to do.

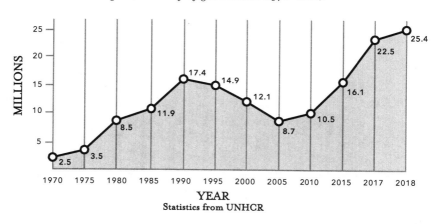

Figure 2: Number of Refugees Worldwide (1970–2018)

Statistics from UNHCR

During my father's imprisonment from 1976–79 in Siem Reap, my Om (Uncle) Chouch took care of my mom, older brother, and myself. With the approval of the Khmer Rouge, my father was allowed to visit us from time to time. Om Chouch had a big family of his own to care for; but he knew if no one cared for us, we would not be able to make it on our own.

Angka—what the Khmer Rouge wanted us to call the government—separated my parents. Angka wanted complete control of our lives: what we thought, what we ate, how we worked, whom we married, and where we lived. During our time in the Pursat camp, when I was only two years old, my older brother, Kim, got sick. My mother went to the person who was responsible for rationing food. She asked if they could give her a little extra for her son. The emotionless reply was "No! It wouldn't be fair to the other families if we gave your son a little more."

Later that night, my older brother looked at the banana leaves hanging above his head and said, "Mom, I'm hungry." Then he fell asleep beside her. The next morning my mother tried to wake him up, but his body was cold and stiff; he died from sickness and starvation. Because I was so young, I didn't know this part of our story until my mother told me when I was in my late teens. There was no way to get the news to my father.

While at the camp in Pursat, my uncle (my father's older brother) was executed in front of my father. Fearing that he would be killed next, my father decided to escape. He weighed his options: "Should I flee to the refugee camp in Thailand or head south to rescue my wife and my two sons?" Heading south would make his trip much longer and increase the risk to his life greatly. But he didn't want to leave without us, so he decided to take the longer and more risky option.

While the Khmer Rouge soldiers were making their rounds in the middle of the night, my father found a makeshift canoe. He hid from the Khmer Rouge in the cover of darkness and headed southward toward Pursat. When he reached my mother and me in our camp, he was heartbroken to hear about the death his oldest son, and he became even more determined to free us from the horrors of living in the camp.

My father begged my mother to leave the camp and head toward Thailand. He went and hid in the woods for a couple of days so that she could get our belongings together and say goodbye to her relatives, knowing that she would never see them again.

While my father was in hiding, the Khmer Rouge came to my mom and asked, "Have you seen your husband?" My mother responded, "I have not seen him." Angka said, "If you are lying to us and we find out, we will execute you and your son." That night, my mother couldn't sleep. She stayed up all night thinking about how she would respond to the Khmer Rouge when they came to question her again. She decided to ask them to take her but to let her son live.

The next morning my father showed up, took my mom and me, and we got into a beat-up rickshaw motorcycle and made the escape to Battambang, Cambodia's second-largest city. I was about three years old. Once we got there, we ran out of money and food. We continued on foot about seventy-two kilometers from Battambang to Srey Sisophon, and then walked another thirty-one kilometers to the Thai border. At night, we tried to sleep in places that were safely removed from the Khmer Rouge, thieves, the Viet Cong, and wild animals. We ate whatever we could find, mostly tree-bark soup with little critters my parents caught on the journey.

In Srey Sisophon, my mother told my dad that she couldn't walk any farther. She had been walking for days and her feet could no longer take it; they were bleeding and throbbing with pain. She told my dad to take me to the refugee camp and let her die there. My dad said that wasn't an option. He wouldn't leave her to die on her own. With exceptional courage, my mother was able to walk a little farther.

When we reached the border, we weren't allowed to enter into the Khao-I-Dang refugee camp, so we had to stay along the refugee camp border. My sister, Channa, was born there and was severely ill. Due to her sickness, the doctors in the camp allowed our family passage into the camp. Once there, my dad pleaded with the doctors and whoever would listen not to send us back into Cambodia; it was too dangerous for us. One of the officials took heed of our pleading and allowed us to live in the camp.

THE REFUGEE CAMP: BIRTH AND DEATH

From 1980 to 1981, we lived in the Khao-I-Dang refugee camp in Sa Kaeo. During that time, the United Nations High Commissioner for Refugees (UNHCR) commissioned my father to teach the written Khmer language to other Cambodian people, which brought in a little income for our family and increased our status in the camp.

My younger brother, Davy, was born in this camp. He was only a year old when he got very sick. My parents took him to see a doctor. A couple of hours later, the doctor came out and said that my brother had died. This sad news devastated my parents. Later that day they took my brother to the local Buddhist temple and had him cremated.

I remember that in the morning I saw my brother in my father's arms, and later that evening they came home without him. It was hard on me. It was hard on all of us. Prior to learning the details of my brother's death, which were only disclosed to me much later, I lived with survival guilt, thinking that I might have been responsible for his death.

My parents first heard about Jesus in this refugee camp. In fact, our next-door neighbors were Jesus people. They shared about Christ with us, but we chose not to believe. How could we? From our perspective, Jesus wasn't there to help us when we were running from the Khmer Rouge and Viet Cong. At that time, Jesus didn't seem real and we couldn't believe that he really cared for us. So we thought.

My aunt, who was living in the United States at that time, had sponsored our immigration process by filling out the papers and submitting them to the authorities. Like many families, my parents would check the community board daily for our family name. The community board would list families who were sponsored to go to France, the US, and other Western countries. After months of waiting, we saw our family name appear on the community board and learned that my aunt had sponsored us to come to the US.

PHILIPPINES REFUGEE PROCESSING CENTER: A BREATH OF FRESH AIR

In the winter of 1981 we boarded a plane and headed to the Morong Bataan refugee processing center near Manila, the capital of the Philippines. After getting off the plane, we rode a crowded bus to the camp. The winding, bumpy road caused us all to feel nauseous, and many people were throwing up. Of course, we knew this was literally our road to freedom. In fact, it felt like an amazing breath of fresh air after years of feeling surrounded by hopelessness and death back in Cambodia and Thailand.

We lived in the Philippines for six months, and during that time I was able to go to a local school for refugee children. Life felt more stable and predictable than before, and I began making new friends. As children, we enjoyed life in this new country without fully realizing our predicament.

While I was there, I met another Cambodian boy who was about my age. We soon became friends and would hang out often and enjoyed playing together. I would come and visit his family's simple home, and they would invite me to have meals with them. Having this stable friendship with this boy and his family helped make me feel secure and established in the community.

It didn't seem so hard to be a refugee in the Philippines. One afternoon when my family and I were napping I got up and found that the door was locked. But to my surprise the door was so thin that I was able to bend it and sneak out of the house without my parents' knowledge. I went to the place where food was being cooked. I was hungry, and I sat there and ate a pot of rice by myself. I was happy and full.

LONG BEACH, CALIFORNIA: HOME AWAY FROM HOME

In the summer of 1982, our family flew to the Los Angeles International Airport. My aunt was supposed to pick us up, but she had the wrong information about our flight and arrival time. After a few hours of waiting at the airport, our sponsor agency took us to the refugee settlement project area in Santa Ana, California. We stayed there for a week until my aunt was able to locate our whereabouts and take us to their one-bedroom apartment. My aunt and uncle had a handful of their own children living in the apartment. It was a tight squeeze, but it was our temporary home away from home.

My first months in America were quite overwhelming. I didn't speak the language and I couldn't understand what was happening around me, be it the busy streets and stores or the unfamiliar music and TV shows. Southeast Asians no longer surrounded me or anything I was accustomed to outside of home. My most vivid memory of American culture was listening to Michael Jackson's albums and learning English by watching *Sesame Street*.

My father was able to find work at Jack in the Box (a burger restaurant) and a donut shop. Once we had enough money saved, we moved to our own little place and bought our first car, a 1981 white Oldsmobile.

INVITATION TO CHURCH:
EXPERIENCING SALVATION AT A CHURCH CAMP

Our family comes from a traditional Buddhist background, and upon our arrival in the United States we had not been to church or heard about salvation through Jesus Christ. But when I was eleven a pastor came to our apartment complex, knocked on our door, and invited our family to church. Although my mother declined, she encouraged the pastor to take her two oldest children—my sister Channa and me—to church. I saw this primarily as a social outing that allowed me to get away from the refugee project area for a while. I made several new friends there and was mentored by pastor Jim Kaufman and Korean missionaries Young and Sue Lee.

When I was fifteen, I was invited to a church youth camp, where I heard about the love of God the Father and Jesus for the first time. Many people at the camp shared testimonies about how Jesus changed their lives. Our pastor shared about the love of Jesus each evening, although I struggled to understand his messages in light of our refugee situation. Then one of the youth leaders asked me about my relationship with my father. Since I didn't have a relationship with my father, that question penetrated deep into my heart. I knew that I hungered for a relationship with some kind of a father figure. Sensing a deep need for a heavenly Father, I cried out loud.

I can say that the realization that God is the heavenly Father I longed for was a defining point in my life. That was when I reached out to God. I felt that, at that point in my life, God comforted me. He allowed me to cry out to him. After that experience, I felt a deep sense of relief and joy in my heart. I felt loved and accepted. Later that year I was baptized at our church, which was the most freeing moment in my life.

A CALL TO MINISTRY

In the years that followed, I met and married a wonderful Thai American woman named Rachel. She shares my love for God and for ministering to others. Also, my father came to Christ. I knew I had a call to ministry, but I worked in a secular environment for many years. In the summer of 2007, Tommy Dyo, the national director of Epic Movement (Campus Crusade for Christ's Asian American Ministry), challenged me to go into full-time ministry. I thought and prayed a lot about it, but struggled with the idea for a long time. I was a supervisor for a printing company, earning a decent living in middle management, so I wasn't sure about quitting my job.

After months of deliberation, in October of 2007 I left my job and went into full-time ministry, trusting God for provision. I can definitely say that he has not failed me yet. He has provided for my financial needs every step of the way. I have grown in my faith and seen amazing provisions in life and ministry these many years.

At first I served with the Asian American Leadership Center as one of its missionaries. I served as director of the Southeast Asian Committee (currently known as the Southeast Asian Catalyst). SEAC desires to see Southeast Asians empowered for church, community, and missional leadership. We have seen hundreds of leaders walk through our doors to be blessed and sent out. In June of 2008, Tom Steers, the director of Asian American Ministries of The Navigators, asked me to come on staff. My heart and mind agreed with The Navigators' vision of reaching, raising, and discipling Asian Americans, with a specific focus on Southeast Asians. Joining The Navigators has been a joyous and life-altering journey for me.

NEW ASSIGNMENT: SOUTHEAST ASIA MINISTRY

My role with The Navigators involves reaching the lost, discipling believers, and building leaders in the Southeast Asian community in North America and in Southeast Asia. I have the joy of serving in diverse settings, including teaching the Long Beach discipleship group, mentoring young men in Filipino ministry, and taking groups back to Southeast Asia so that they can share the love of Christ with their family and friends who still live there.

In 2006, God spoke to my heart about Cambodia at a Navigators retreat. One of the speakers talked about the kingdom of God and described many key principles from the Scriptures about organically reaching pre-believers by focusing on families. And when he showed us a map of the world, Cambodia stood out to me with a new burden for my relatives there. I started visiting Cambodia and meeting with extended family members. My father joins me on these trips and is effective in sharing about Jesus on account of his language fluency. We share our stories and pray with our family members. We have gone from village to village and seen many come to faith during these trips. As a father-son team, we have been able to visit many villages in Cambodia every year since 2010; and God has birthed six house churches. These groups meet regularly in homes to pray, study the Bible, and share Jesus with others in their village.

In 1982, my father and I left Cambodia not knowing if we would ever return. We left Cambodia as Buddhists, and we found Jesus in America. God reconciled us to each other and called us to go back to Cambodia with the message of redemption and reconciliation in the context of our family. Rachel and I are waiting on God to be sent as missionaries to Cambodia and Thailand. As long as I am alive, my passion is to see Southeast Asians come to a loving and lasting relationship with Jesus Christ.

chapter two

Three Times a Refugee: Journey of an Afghani Doctor

DR. AHMAD KARIM

"Excuse me—may I ask you where you got that iron?"

Gently grabbing the man's arm, I raised the question. Our refugee family had just arrived in Chicago from Afghanistan. Now my sons and I were beginning to gather a few household items. My wife had asked for an iron, but we didn't know where any of the shops were. As I stood in a neighborhood market, surrounded by a bewildering array of material goods, I spotted an iron—in the hand of another customer. He also had two young boys with him, who appeared to be his sons. So I gathered courage, pushed forward, and asked where he found the iron.

"Do you need an iron?" the man asked. His two boys watched and listened.

"Yes," I answered, "my wife wants me to buy one."

"You can take this one." The man smiled and handed the iron to me.

"But if you give it to me, what will you say to *your* wife if you are supposed to bring home an iron?" I protested.

"When my wife hears that I gave it to a refugee, she will be more than happy," the man answered.

His name was Pastor Bob, I learned as we continued to talk. To me this was even more important than the iron. Our family had become Christians during our refugee journey through Pakistan and India. When we finally arrived in Chicago, we really missed the church we had attended in India. Although there was a thirteen-hour time difference, and it was past midnight in India while it was three in the afternoon in Chicago, I called my church there.

"I'm sorry to bother you at this late hour, but I missed my church this Sunday," I said over the phone. "Will you please pray for me that I can join a church next Sunday? How can I contact a church family in Chicago? We don't have internet here yet. But God is the same God everywhere. Please pray for me."

They did. "Dear God, please help Dr. Karim find a church in Chicago as soon as possible," I heard them praying through my mobile phone.

Now here was Pastor Bob, the pastor of New Hope Community Church, holding an iron.

Pastor Bob came to the rented room where we were housed. He saw how dark it was, with hardly any lights. Pretty soon he returned with a portable lamp. The next day Pastor Bob brought his car and drove me to his church so that I could see that it wasn't far.

Arriving in the US had exceeded our imaginations. We had prayed, and now we could hardly believe that we were here. For three nights in transit we had not slept because we were so excited. Then, when we stepped off of the airplane, people were so kind. "Hello. Are you tired?" they greeted us. They helped us with our suitcases. Everyone showed us respect, and also where to eat and stay. They brought us blankets and kitchen utensils and even flowers. On our first day at a hotel, five people came to welcome us with food and gifts.

But better than all that was meeting Pastor Bob. How marvelous to experience God's family in a new place. I had called my church in India and asked them to pray that God would show me the way, because I didn't know where to go. Then in the market, even though I knew it was discourteous to grab someone's arm, I did it anyway; and God connected us. God is the same God everywhere. By means of an object as simple as an iron, we found Christian fellowship in our new homeland.

MY LIFE JOURNEY

I was born at the top of the world, if altitude is the measure. A great wall of snow-capped giants extends from the Karakorum Mountains all the way through the Hindu Kush, Tien Shan, and Himalayan ranges, including some of the highest summits on earth.

Afghanistan also has a long heritage of art, culture, and palaces—and Christian faith. A thousand years ago Afghanistan was home to many Christians. Coins from that era bear the inscription "In the name of the Father, Son and Holy Ghost, one God." Ancient carpet patterns are decorated with crosses. The monuments and ruins of cloisters testify to flourishing seminaries and mission-training schools. Today, however, there are forty-eight thousand mosques but not a single church building in Afghanistan.

Figure 3: Top Refugee-hosting Countries in the World (2016)

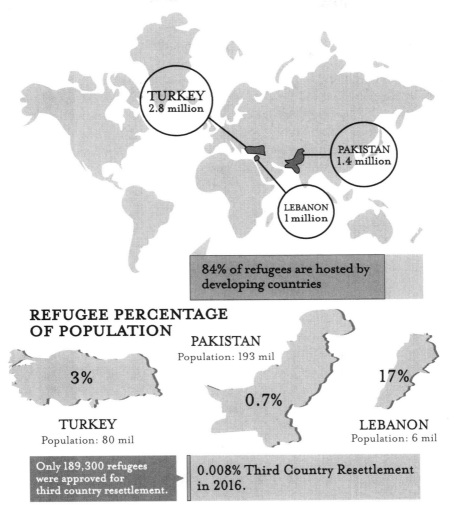

REFUGEE PERCENTAGE OF POPULATION

84% of refugees are hosted by developing countries

TURKEY
2.8 million

PAKISTAN
1.4 million

LEBANON
1 million

PAKISTAN
Population: 193 mil

3%

0.7%

17%

TURKEY
Population: 80 mil

LEBANON
Population: 6 mil

Only 189,300 refugees were approved for third country resettlement.

0.008% Third Country Resettlement in 2016.

Though I was originally from Kandahar, I went to Kabul to study. There I got married and became a medical doctor and eventually a professor in the medical school where I had studied. However, in 1978 the Russians invaded Afghanistan. There was no well-functioning Afghani government at that time. All men were forced to join the army. Our family decided to move across the border to a refugee camp in Pakistan. We built a house, and I set up a clinic. There we lived and worked for the next twenty years. My daughter was born and educated there. All of my patients were Afghan refugees from back home.

Conditions improved in Afghanistan over the next two decades; so after the Russians left and the power of the Taliban declined, we moved back home. There were new job opportunities with good salaries. I worked for different NGOs, which had its pros and cons financially. If a doctor worked for the national health system, it came with a retirement package. NGOs connected with the United Nations did not offer pensions, but they paid five to ten times more than the government. During these years I changed fields from general practitioner to ultrasound specialist. We were enjoying a pleasant and comfortable life, with a large home and a fine car.

Tragically, the Taliban revived again and life became very dangerous. In a country with forbidding terrain, few roads, and a tradition of fierce values, warlords ruled their own regions. Weapons had always been important, but now there were even more, including the weapons left by the Soviets when they fled and the weapons imported to arm those who fought the Soviets. Poverty was widespread. Four million orphans, the refuse of war, scrambled just to eat. Wealth often traveled illegal routes, since 90 percent of the world's opium poppies grew here. The next generation longed for something better. As young men listened to the Taliban and joined the cause, its power grew stronger.

The Taliban objected to professionals working with foreign partners. Sometimes they also attacked those who worked for the government. This included the staff of hospitals and clinics. I was working with the International Medical Corp, which had British ties. As the Taliban grew stronger, their violence increased. One day in June of 2012, members of the Taliban came for one of my colleagues. Like many of us, he had a private clinic in his home. He worked there after he finished his shift at the hospital. When the Taliban knocked on his door, he assumed they were patients seeking help. He opened the door, and the armed men came in and cut off his head. Then they just left his head sitting there on the table in the front room of his office. Why? Because he worked with the government.

Over the previous months I had been warned that my name might be on the Taliban's list. One seventy-year-old lady in my neighborhood had hypertension. Whenever her mood changed, she would call for me, even at midnight. "Please check on me." She also came periodically to the clinic in my house. She had four sons, who may have been with the Taliban. She warned me, "It's better if you change your address, if you move away from here. You don't need to continue working here. The Taliban cohort has argued about you, and I think you are on the list of people to be killed."

But I had a good salary and a settled life. How much could an old woman know?

Two days after my colleague's dreadful beheading, the Taliban came for me. They came to my home at 1:00 a.m. For an hour and a half they terrorized and tortured my family. I cannot talk about that night. I cry if I start to tell it.

We fled the country, leaving everything. I had an ultrasound machine worth $600,000 that I gave up. My car, which I had bought for $20,000, I sold for $5,000. I sold my house for $115,000, although it had cost three times more than that.

We moved to India, and once again began to rebuild our lives. I had a certificate from the International Medical Corp. and was able treat other Afghans, but I was unable to develop a clinic. Korean missionaries paid me a salary and also provided food for our family. In my spare time in India, I developed the skills to become a chess champion on the computer.

"I'M LONELY"

My daughter felt lonely in India. "I feel alone," she said. "There is no one here that I feel close to. Please, I need contact with some other Afghans."

This longing led our family not only to fellow Afghans but also to the Lord Jesus Christ.

I began to ask around. "I want to meet some Afghans. Where could I find some?"

Then I encountered someone who asked me a surprising question. "Do you want to have a hundred Afghans come to your house?"

"How?" I wondered.

"There is a Christian church of Afghans here," he answered.

I went to the church gathering to see what it was like. I discovered that they were like a family—so nice, and so interested in us. There were Bible studies in different people's homes. There was both a Sunday and a Saturday worship meeting. It was all very interesting. I started taking their training classes. Although I was a doctor and a professor, I became a student. We were beginners in spiritual works, like how to pray. But I came to believe there was a way of living that was better than Islam. So I changed.

This church was started by Koreans who had been expelled from Afghanistan. When they realized they couldn't continue their ministry in Afghanistan, they transferred to New Delhi and began reaching out to the Afghans there. Two Korean women were the mainstays. Because we couldn't remember their Korean names, we changed them to Aisha and Maryam. Maryam tutored my daughter in English. Four or five times a year people from Korea or other countries would come to visit our church.

After we believed in Jesus, we had to take courses for two months. Only then were we baptized. When I had worked in the hospital in Afghanistan, there had been a few Christian patients. Observing them, I had thought that Christianity is just for super people—people with a car and a good income—not ordinary people like us. In New Delhi, however, I saw that Jesus is for everybody. The Christians exuded a deep sense of joy and peace in spite of their condition. I began to long for that.

Eventually I began to write spiritual songs for the church. Working with another writer and composer, we completed a Pushto hymnbook. We created these songs because singing in English is not enough. It's better to speak five words in a language that people know than to speak five thousand words in a language they don't know.

As I reflected on spiritual living, I remembered our time in Pakistan. There I had felt pressured to pray five times a day. But it had seemed hypocritical to me. It reminded me of a joke about a chicken.

A boy stole a chicken and shoved it under his wraparound blanket. The owner of the chicken saw that the boy had the chicken under his clothes.

"Why did you steal my chicken?" she asked.

"Believe me, I did not steal it," he protested.

"But why do I see the feet of my chicken sticking out from under your shirt?"

When I was in Pakistan, the Taliban and other Muslims said that they never stole the chicken. But I saw the feet of the chicken. They were saying one thing, but doing something else.

By contrast, the people in the church in New Delhi were honest. They were a very strange and interesting family. They showed concern for us. If my wife had a headache, they would call to ask, "How is your wife? How are you?" That's like a family with genuine concerns.

They also enjoyed fun times, like swimming and dancing. They were fellow Afghanis, but different and a better kind of people. The only way to explain the transformation is their encounter with Jesus. There are twenty-five thousand Afghans in New Delhi, and there are no restrictions on being Christian or Muslim. Although I have landed in a good place here in America, I cannot forget about the people who first introduced me to Jesus Christ and taught me to be a follower of him.

chapter three

Sustaining Karen Refugee Community in Oakland

STEVEN ROZZI AND RUSSELL JEUNG, PHD

After his village in the Karen state of Burma was burned by the military, Saw Khu Gey and his family spent ten years in refugee camps in Southeast Asia before resettling in California. Though he has been in the United States longer than many of his compatriots, he struggles to learn English, preventing him from adjusting fully to life in Oakland. He somberly observed,

> When we get here, the most difficult thing that we face is the language barrier because we don't understand or speak English. Everywhere we go we have to go with someone who speaks or can translate for us. Sometimes we don't know how to get from one place to another. Everywhere we go—social services or the hospital or anywhere we go—we worry about interpretation because sometimes they don't provide interpreters.

Saw Khu Gey comes from a very remote part of Burma; his lack of access to formal education when he was growing up continues to hinder his ability to learn English. Health issues also prevent him from attending classes, since he has difficulty walking. Despite these obstacles, he hopes to "simply be able to speak English. One day I want to understand people even though I can't read or write anything. I hope one day I can reply to people." Fleeing their homes due to political, ethnic, and religious oppression, more than 140,000 Burmese refugees have settled in the United States since 2007. Coming to the US offers them new opportunities, but also poses many new challenges. This chapter outlines some of the difficulties facing Karen refugees in Oakland, California, and some efforts taken to alleviate them.[1]

HISTORY OF THE KAREN PEOPLE

Since the independence of Burma (now known as Myanmar) in 1948, government officials have persecuted ethnic and religious minority groups such as the Karen, Karenni, Muslims, and Christians. Insurgent groups have since challenged state oppression, especially after a military coup in 1962 and the military regime declared Buddhism as the state religion, leading to violence against religious minorities. After suppression of a pro-democracy movement in 1988, which led to more than three thousand civilian deaths, members of Burmese ethnic states sought refugee status. In 1990 the military junta denied the electoral victory of a democratically elected president, Aung San Suu Kyi, and remained in power. In 2008 Cyclone Nargis hit Burma, killing 138,000 people and displacing 2.4 million more, while the ruling junta offered little support.

Beginning in 2010 the Burmese government, embroiled in multiple violent conflicts with its residents, began reforms to move the country toward a more liberal democracy. Burma held its first elections in 2015, and the National League for Democracy (led by Aung San Suu Kyi) won in a landslide and established the first civilian president in power since 1962. However, Burma continues to abuse religious minorities through violence against places of worship, forced conversions, and restrictions on land ownership.[2]

Due to dire economic and political conditions, Burma remains one of the poorest countries in the world. Nearly 1.5 million people (2.5 percent of the population) are displaced in Burma, and millions have sought asylum in foreign countries. Thailand received most of these refugees, with nine refugee camps near its border hosting over 2 million, while the United States accepted around 18,000 Burmese refugees in 2015, 12,000 in 2016, and expected to take in

---

1 Much of this chapter is derived from the report "From Crisis to Community," which uses data gathered from 194 surveys, twelve in-depth interviews, and two focus groups with a diverse group of refugees from Burma. Participants came from a variety of Burmese ethnic backgrounds: Karen (43 percent), Karenni (29 percent), Burman (14 percent), Muslims (3 percent), Rakhaing (2 percent), and Kachin (2 percent). Religiously, 46 percent of respondents identify with Protestant Christianity, 25 percent with Buddhism, 17 percent with Roman Catholicism, and 8 percent with ancestor veneration. This group ranged in age as well: 31–40 years old (28 percent), 41–50 years old (27 percent), 51–60 years old (21 percent), and 21–30 years old (13 percent). Four out of five refugees arrived since 2007: 34 percent in 2009, 22 percent in 2008, and 15 percent in 2007.

2 Rachel Fleming, *Hidden Plight: Christian Minorities in Burma* (U.S. Commission on International Religious Freedom, 2016), www.uscirf.gov/sites/default/files/Hidden%20Plight.%20Christian%20Minorities%20in%20Burma.pdf (accessed October 1, 2017).

another 5,000 in 2017. Since 2007, more refugees have arrived in the United States from Burma than from any other country in the world.[3] Other countries hosting Burmese refugees include Malaysia, Singapore, and Indonesia. Over a million people are internally displaced, most of whom are from Christian areas in Burma.

Figure 4: Most Congested Refugee Routes in the World

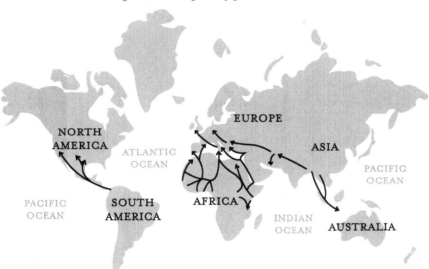

For much of Burma's post-independence history, Karens residing in the eastern state of Karen have faced the brunt of the violence and oppression from the central government. While six million Karens live in Burma (7 percent of the total population), more than one million reside in refugee camps in neighboring Thailand and out of 168,000 Burmese refugees in the United States in 2015, nearly half are from the Karen state and nearly 95% of Karen refugees in the US are Christians.[4] Unlike other ethnic groups in Burma, many Karens became Christians after the arrival of Baptist missionaries in 1826.[5]After the nation gained independence, ethnic tensions rose and police killed eighty Karen Christians celebrating Christmas in the small village of

---

3 "Annual Refugee Arrivals into the U.S. by Nationality," Pew Research Center, http://www.pewglobal. org/2017/10/12/appendix-b-detailed-data-tables-u-s-refugees/ (accessed October 1, 2017).

4 "Burmese in the US: Fact Sheet" Pew Social Trends. http://www.pewsocialtrends.org/fact-sheet/asian-americans-burmese-in-the-u-s/ (accessed Jul 1, 2018) and Karen Refugees from Burma – Minnesota Dept. of Health http://www.health.state.mn.us/divs/idepc/refugee/karenref09.pdf (accessed Jul 1, 2018).

5 Kwanchewan Buadaeng, "Ethnic Identities of the Karen Peoples in Burma and Thailand," in *Identity Matters: Ethnic and Sectarian Conflict*, ed. James L. Peacock, Patricia M. Thornton, and Patrick B. Inman (New York: Berghahn Books, 2007), 73–94.

Palaw in southern Burma. This event triggered the ongoing violence between Karen and the Burmese government, along with many Karen Christians fleeing to Thailand. Though ceasefire agreements have been made between Karen and the Burmese government, violence continues in the region.

RESETTLEMENT CHALLENGES FOR
KAREN REFUGEES IN OAKLAND

Alameda County, which includes the city of Oakland, ranks second among California counties in hosting refugees from Burma, having accepted 494 refugees between 1995 and 2015. Refugees arriving in Oakland lack English proficiency and job skills, which exacerbates all issues associated with resettlement. The city and county's overall poverty and lack of tax base contribute to poor schools and fewer nonprofit services. Moreover, the growing gentrification has displaced the poor from their homes in Oakland, and inadequate police staffing and poor police-community relations results in high crime rates.

ENGLISH LANGUAGE BARRIERS

Since Burmese refugees have arrived, the city of Oakland has faced a number of difficulties, including a budget deficit during the recession of 2007–10 and multiple transitions in public school leadership (eight superintendents in the last sixteen years). Many public schools in Oakland are underfunded due to high staffing and administrative costs. Thus refugees and their children face a major hurdle in their pressing need to acquire English language proficiency. Forty-six percent of Oakland's public school students do not meet state standards in English, compared to the state average of 28 percent. Further, the school district ended many of its adult ESL programs during the recession. Although classes returned in 2011, the number of schools offering programs decreased from fifteen in 2011 to only six in 2015, while the number of participants in these classes shrank from 410 to 290 in the same period.

Very few Burmese refugees (14 percent) report being able to speak English well. Over 65 percent of Burmans (another ethnic group) speak English, while only 40 percent of Karen do. Their lack of English skills inhibits their adaptation to the United States by preventing them from obtaining employment and securing adequate health care; and it keeps them socially isolated in their host country. Many refugees in our survey identified learning English as one of their greatest needs and key to gaining employment. Those who cannot speak, read, or write English are at a great disadvantage in the American society.

For example, after being orphaned at age eleven and spending nineteen years in a refugee camp, Haw Reh now lives in Oakland with his wife and two adult sons but remains unemployed. Recognizing his need to learn English, he debates the value of staying in the United States:

> Since we can't speak English, how can we get a job? I only worry about the rent. If I had a job, life here would be better than the refugee camp, because we have a house and I could pay the bills. But since I have no job, I would rather go back to living in the refugee camp.

Indeed, English barriers make surmounting other challenges, such as securing stable employment and access to government services, almost impossible without outside support.

POVERTY AND STATE SUPPORT

Even if refugees learn English, their poverty status and gentrification make Oakland an increasingly difficult place in which to live. Even with initial subsidies, almost 90 percent of refugees from Burma in Oakland live under the federal poverty line and end up unemployed because of the lack of available job training. Compared to the national refugee unemployment rate of 46 percent, the jobless rate of Karen refugees in Oakland, at 64 percent, is much higher. Among the unemployed, 75 percent earn less than $2,000 a year, designating them as "extremely poor" by federal standards. Those with jobs often earn the minimum wage, which is just over $13 an hour in Oakland, and have limited working hours. A living wage that can fully support two adults and a child in Oakland is over $30 an hour.

The high cost of living in Oakland creates further great strain for refugees in poverty. Between 2011 and 2017, the median rent for a two-bedroom apartment in Oakland increased 64 percent, from $2,115 to $3,264 per month. With nine of ten of refugees earning less than $2,200 a month, they have very few housing options. As refugees from Burma have typically resettled a number of times already before moving to Oakland, they face the prospect of being pushed out of their homes yet again due to economic factors.[66]

The repeated uprooting and displacing creates much insecurity and fear, affecting even their children's psychological well-being. For example, Yim Win Moe can only obtain seasonal work that does not cover her expenses. Living in Oakland for two years after leaving her two children with her parents in Burma,

---

6 Russell Jeung, "Uprooted Again: Internally Displaced Refugees in the United States," *Evangelicals for Social Action*, April 2017, http://www.evangelicalsforsocialaction.org/faith-and-public-life/uprooted-again-internally-displaced-refugees-in-the-united-states/ (accessed July 8, 2017).

she reflects on the difficulties of earning an adequate income and coping with her subsequent stress:

> I work very hard but at times, there is not enough money. Sometimes I work three days a week. At other times, I work two days a week. Once in a while, my paycheck does not cover the rent. . . . At times I get depressed. I have friends who are able to help me, but if I were to rely on government, it would be very difficult.

The small government assistance offered to refugees is not enough to surmount the high cost of living in Oakland. Refugee Cash Assistance (RCA), received by 21 percent of refugees, is only offered for eight months. Only one in five refugees obtains benefits from the CalWorks program when their RCA runs out. Without enough resources to provide for basic needs, many refugees are unable to adequately address the health and safety issues often present in impoverished communities.

SAFETY AND HEALTH

Residing in areas with high poverty, refugees in Oakland face both crime and poor health. With 168 violent crimes and 594 property crimes per ten thousand residents, Oakland is much more dangerous than most other cities in California. Most Burmese refugees live in East Oakland, which is considered the crime capital of the state. And when refugees are victimized by crime, they are often left with little recourse. Saw Mu Ler, a Karen community organizer, noted the specific vulnerability of refugees in Oakland:

In my opinion, [criminals] target refugees because they can do it to this particular group of people. Robbers know that the refugees don't speak English, they can't tell the police who are the perpetrators. So the police won't be able to find the robbers.

Besides physical dangers, refugees face the threat of poor health. Due to lack of access to health care in their home country, refugees often present complicated health issues requiring long-term care. Many Karen refugees (60 percent) cited language or lack of translators as the principal barrier to accessing health care in spite of having health insurance. The refugees suffer mental health challenges on account of war-related trauma, displacement stress, international refugee resettlement, and living in high-crime neighborhoods. Seventy-two percent of refugees from Burma reported emotional issues and stress-related symptoms such as headaches, depression, or sleeping difficulties that hinder their ability to work or care for family. Household problems such as alcoholism, marital conflicts, and domestic violence are widespread. Many suffer from anxiety disorders, loss of identity, acculturation stress, family breakdown, and lack of a support system, as well as many other psychological troubles. And because of the social taboo associated with mental ailments, Karen refugees in Oakland are less likely to admit emotional or relational woes and to seek help from mental health professionals.

GOD AT WORK AMONG KAREN REFUGEES IN OAKLAND

Witnessing the difficulties facing refugees from Burma, New Hope Covenant Church in Oakland partnered with the Burma Family Refugee Network (BRFN) and Asian Health Services (AHS) from 2010 through 2012 to develop a strategic plan for the community. Together these groups organized a series of health fairs that drew refugees to complete needs-assessment surveys and receive health care. The resulting report, "From Crisis to Community Development," was instrumental in garnering over $600,000 in funding for employment and health programs. BRFN helps to coordinate employment services for all refugees, and AHS has hired Karen-speaking health navigators for the community. From making appointments to learning how to follow medical treatments and dosages, these navigators guide Karen refugees through the process of taking care of their own health.

Further supporting the healthy adaptation of refugees from Burma, New Hope and KCFC have long prayed for meaningful work opportunities for refugees. Several local businesses have emerged that are employing refugees with high wages. Volunteers from New Hope and Karen Christian Fellowship assist refugees in setting up interviews, training them for their new work environment, and orienting them to their rights as workers.

In adjusting to their new home, children of refugees often distance themselves from their home culture and language, creating tension between themselves and their parents. In an effort to resolve these issues, KCFC has organized a Karen language school for children. Volunteers teach children to read, sing, and memorize Bible verses in Karen. The school helps to improve family relations, reinforce their ethnic identity in the face of marginalization, and provide structured extracurricular activities.

Pastor Aye Thaw, who has led KCFC since 2000, acts as a key community advocate for the Karen in Oakland as they become accustomed to life in California. She connects them with job opportunities, interprets during hospital visits, and assists refugee families as they resettle. Reflecting on her congregation, which now consists of over one hundred members, she hopes that the Karen in Oakland will become a part of the fabric of their community: "I want them to become real good citizens of this country, where they can speak English well and have a good job. That is my biggest hope."

Pastor Aye Thaw is especially grateful for the long partnership that has formed between her church and volunteers from New Hope Covenant Church:

> They really care and they really love our people. . . . It's very good for us and we're very grateful for their part. As Jesus said, you need to care for the poor people—not only the physically poor, but the spiritually poor also. That's why we are very joyful and we love to work with them.

New Hope members also benefit from supporting a Karen-refugee church. Facing the common issues of a middle-class American church—slow growth and spiritual stagnation—the church recognizes the value of serving Karen refugees. A New Hope member describes the joy he gets from partnering with KCFC:

> Joining with these kids and their families gets me out of my own self-obsession. Having others to care for frees me from my own small preoccupations, as their struggles become my struggles and their joy becomes my joy.

In connecting with Karen refugees, Christians receive a fresh experience of their faith among those who have experienced an arduous journey of refugee displacements. The presence of new Christians in any church has profound impact on the faith of seasoned, pew-warming churchgoers. In fact, churches involved with refugees end up receiving much more spiritually from refugees in return for their material gifts and practice of hospitality.

CONCLUSION

Escaping political and religious persecution in their home country, Karen refugees are creating a community for themselves in Oakland. Though they face great obstacles, such as learning English, escaping poverty, and overcoming poor health, Karens are overcoming them with the help of local churches and agencies. While the city of Oakland faces its own issues in supporting its vulnerable populations, Karens continue to work together to succeed in school, find sustainable work, and hold on to ethnic and family identities. Karen Christians find help in American churches such as New Hope, which ease their transition and encourage their faith. Church partnership provides both Karen and American Christians with a tangible expression of faith, as people who were once strangers are welcomed into a new home.

chapter four

Jordan, Home for Refugees: Two Challenges

J. Wu, PhD

"I would like to thank God for this journey, this migration. And I would like to thank ISIS!"

What strange words to come from the man on the platform. Like a lightning bolt they jolted the church members.

Who was this speaker? He was an Iraqi who had fled to Jordan with his family. When they first arrived, they were depressed. They rarely smiled. Their shoulders sagged. They had little energy. But a local church welcomed them and bathed them with love and care. Then, as weeks passed, according to one church member, "We saw a change in them. They became more joyful, always excited to greet us."

Now the time had come for them to move on. The family had been granted asylum in Australia. As they prepared to leave, the father went to the front of the church and gave a testimony in Arabic. That is when he thanked ISIS.

"Two years ago, when ISIS invaded our hometown of Mosul, I was far from God," he said. "I am from a Christian family, but I did not know Jesus. But here in this country, in this church, I found Jesus. I discovered God's Word. When I came here, I had nothing, and now I have everything. I was poor, and now I am rich! So I thank ISIS for what they did, and I thank this church for helping me find Jesus."

This man is part of a great movement of people into Jordan. Violence in the Middle East has flooded Jordan with Syrian, Iraqi, and Yemeni refugees, in addition to displaced Palestinians. This chapter will explore Jordan's history, the current refugee crisis, what local churches are doing to help, and two challenges requiring attention.

HISTORICAL CONTEXT

The country of Jordan has been known as a home for refugees. Over half of Jordan's residents are refugees or their descendants. The first wave came from Palestine in 1948, when the nation of Israel was established. More Palestinian refugees came in 1967 because of the Six-Day War, and still more in 1990 because of the Gulf War. Today Jordan remains the country hosting the largest Palestinian diaspora outside of the Palestinian territories. As many as 4.4 million residents in the kingdom of Jordan have Palestinian ancestry.[1]

Many Palestinians have been naturalized and have received Jordanian citizenship. The latest census, in 2015, didn't even ask for nor specify the Palestinian ancestry of Jordanian citizens (whether originally Palestinian or Jordanian). However, some Palestinians have not received citizenship, and the 2015 census notes more than six hundred thousand in the kingdom who continue to be identified by Palestinian identity documents.[2]

During the 2003 Iraq War, a flood of Iraqi refugees arrived in Jordan. The beginning of the civil war in Syria in 2011 brought a steady stream of Syrian refugees to Jordan. In 2014, the invasion of Mosul by ISIS and the civil war in Yemen both propelled smaller groups of Iraqis and Yemenis to Jordan. As per the 2015 census, out of 9.5 million residents in Jordan, 1.3 million are refugees (not including the original Palestinian refugees).[3] Along with Syria, Iraq, Lebanon, Palestine, and Egypt, Jordan hosts a Christian minority, most of whom are traditional Orthodox or Catholics. Taken all together, Christians made up about 2.2 percent of the Jordanian population in 2016. The evangelical spiritual revival among traditional Christians began in the early 1930s through ministries like that of Rev. Roy Whitman. After Palestinian refugees arrived in the late 1940s, other evangelical ministries expanded through denominations such as the Nazarene Church, the Assemblies of God, the Christian and Missionary Alliance, and the Southern Baptist Convention.

Christians in Jordan—that is, those born in Christian families to Christian parents—have the freedom to worship and observe Christian holidays. But according to the law of the land, those who proselytize Muslims may be prosecuted in the State Security Court under the penal code's provisions against "inciting sectarian conflict" or "harming the national unity." Although the constitution does not explicitly forbid Muslims from leaving their religion,

---

1 Minorities at Risk Project, University of Maryland, https://web.archive.org/web/20160101101403/ http://www.cidcm.umd.edu/mar/assessment.asp?groupId=66302 (accessed in October 2017).

2 Jordan's "General Results of Census 2015," http://www.dos.gov.jo/dos_home_e/main/population/ census2015/index.htm (accessed in October 2017).

3 Ibid. The total number of non-Jordanian citizens residing in Jordan is 2.9 million.

"The constitution and the law accord primacy to *sharia*, which prohibits Muslims from converting to another religion. Under *sharia*, converts from Islam are still considered Muslims but regarded as apostates." Muslims who convert usually suffer isolation, persecution, and in more radical cases, death at the hands of their family and society.

Figure 5: Eastern Mediterranean Refugee Routes

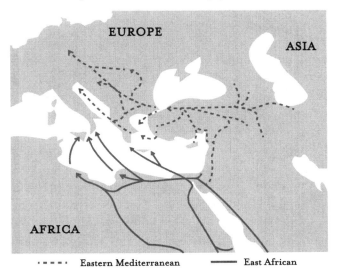

•—■—■—• Eastern Mediterranean   ——— East African

CURRENT REFUGEE WORK

As of September 2017, UNHCR reports 733,607 registered refugees in Jordan (not including Palestinian refugees): 654,213 Syrians, 64,535 Iraqis, 8,464 Yemeni, and 3,905 Sudanese. Only 19 percent of these refugees live in refugee camps.[4] However, the 2015 Jordanian census reports more than 950,000 Syrian refugees living in Jordan, suggesting a large number of refugees who did not register with the UN.[5]

The vast influx of refugees has had a significant impact on the economy and life of local Jordanians. An all-around rise in prices followed the wave of Iraqi refugees from the 2003 Gulf War. Jordan has yet to recover from this. As a rule, refugees are not allowed to work without a work permit. In 2016 the Jordanian

---

4 "Jordan Operational Update," UNHCR, September 2017, https://reliefweb.int/sites/reliefweb.int/files/resources/Jordan%20Operational%20Update%20September%202017.pdf (accessed in October 2017).

5 The total number of Syrians living in Jordan, including nonrefugees who came before the war, is given at 1.2 million. Jordan's "General Results of Census 2015," http://www.dos.gov.jo/dos_home_e/main/population/census2015/index.htm (accessed October 2017).

Ministry of Labor started issuing more work permits to Syrian refugees, totaling more than twenty-five thousand from January to August 2016.[6]

Local people I encounter generally express sympathy for refugees, whereas the Syrian refugee families I visit complain about ill treatment from locals. Recent studies support these perceptions. According to a World Health Organization 2013 report[7], 95 percent of Syrian refugees have received help from community-based organizations (CBOs), which includes local Islamic charity associations (jama'iat). Some female refugees reported that they were asked for sexual favors in exchange for services.

Education is another concern. According to the United Nations estimates more than half of Syrian refugee children (five to seventeen year olds) are not enrolled in school[8]. To cope with this problem, the Jordanian Ministry of Education has created double-shift schools and catch-up centers for refugee children. Such schools usually receive Jordanian students in the morning and Syrian students in the afternoon. Still, Syrian refugee families complain about the low quality of education and poor treatment from Jordanian teachers. Generations For Peace Institute also reports ill treatment of Syrian refugees in urban settings and in schools.

In this context, Jordanian churches serve refugees through educational, medical, and relief and development services. A Christian hospital in northern Jordan does meaningful ministry among Syrian refugees and other Middle Eastern migrants. The government has been relatively tolerant of their witness due to their significant contribution to the community. A few local churches in that region, including one Catholic and several evangelical congregations, distribute food packages to refugees, visit them at home, and provide informal education to their children. Some churches in the capital, Amman, offer adult English classes for Iraqi and Syrian refugees. Some of these classes are free, while others charge very minimal tuition. From a base in Amman, a church has started informal schools in two northern villages. These schools open doors for Christians to visit the refugee students' families. Some faith-based organizations and local churches have developed business projects in which refugees make and sell handmade items and local food products. This enables refugees to support themselves in part, while also cultivating life skills.

---

6 "Refugee Livelihoods: Jordan," UNHCR,
   https://reliefweb.int/sites/reliefweb.int/files/resources/
   UNHCRThematicUpdateLivelihoodsSeptember2017_0.pdf (accessed October 2017).
7 http://www.who.int/hac/Syria_regional_response_plan_june2013.pdf (accessed Jul 21, 2017)
8 Educational and Mental Health Needs of Syrian Refugee Children, Migration Policy Institute report Oct 2015 Pg 8. www.migrationpolicy.org/sites/default/files/publications/FCD-Sirin-Rogers-
   FINAL.pdf (accessed Jul 1, 2017)

When my coworkers and I visit Syrian families, we take food packages and other relief items. We also listen to their stories and ask about their needs. Many have family members who are missing or who have been killed back home. Despite this heartbreaking situation, they show hospitality eagerly, serving tea or coffee to their guests. However, we have not encountered any Syrian refugees who desire to remain in Jordan. They desire either to immigrate to Western countries or to return to Syria.

While most Syrian refugees in Jordan are Muslims, Iraqi refugees include a population of Christians.[9] Evangelistic and discipling ministries among the latter have borne fruit. When Iraqi Christians flee from ISIS to Jordan, churches in Jordan—Orthodox, Catholic, and evangelical—provide material support to these newcomers. Most of these refugees are from nominal, traditional Christian backgrounds. It is quite common for these families to attend multiple churches in order to receive more relief or cash.

Compared with Syrian refugees, Iraqi refugees are better off, most of them being from middle-class families. Many fled from ISIS in Mosul in 2014. Others emigrated from Baghdad more recently, feeling that Iraq is unstable, with hostile attitudes toward Christians that are only getting worse. These Iraqi Christian refugees do not desire to go back to Iraq, but instead hope to immigrate to a Western country. Many eventually are granted asylum, often to Australia.

Some local evangelical churches, including one that I have served with, are experiencing fruitful, life-transforming ministry among these Iraqi Christian refugees, successfully making disciples of these cultural Christians. Church members visit them regularly in their homes, teaching them the Word of God. Many have never read the Bible before. Through loving care and teaching, quite a few have become true believers. The Iraqi man who thanked ISIS is one example.

MINISTRY CHALLENGES

Alongside of many encouraging reports of these ministries in Jordan, there are numerous challenges involved in ministering to refugees. Two of these challenges are (1) pressure from the government and fear of persecution, and (2) foreign money and the local church.

---

9 There are also Syrian Christian refugees, but they have tended to seek refuge in Lebanon, likely due to religious and political reasons, since Lebanon is not a Muslim country.

PRESSURE FROM THE GOVERNMENT AND FEAR OF PERSECUTION

The government's security apparatus monitors evangelistic efforts in the country. Although Jordan is a close ally of Western countries, presenting itself as highly valuing human rights and religious freedom, local culture and public opinion do not always fully embrace these values. To appease Islamic religious leaders, and to protect the Christian community from being targeted by Islamist militants, the government has made an effort to prevent public proselytizing activities and mass conversions. Local church leaders have been interrogated by security police, foreign missionaries have been asked to leave the country, and believers from Muslim background at times have been beaten or put in jail.

On the other hand, the government also protects the safety and religious freedom of Christians. After a terrorist attack in the southern city of Karak in December 2016, the government canceled all outdoor Christmas celebration events in Jordan, while increasing police force presence to protect Christmas and New Year's church services. Ever since Syrian refugees began coming to Jordan in 2012, a few local churches have been trying to reach out to them. However, many of the local churches are afraid of harassment from the security police, so they don't want to get involved. By contrast, sharing the gospel with Christian Iraqi refugees is not viewed as a security threat. Therefore, churches feel freer to evangelize and disciple these refugees. In general, Jordanian Christians do not want to be seen as troublemakers in society. As a religious minority group who has suffered from discrimination, they rely on the protection of the regime.

FOREIGN MONEY AND THE LOCAL CHURCH

The refugee crisis has made front-page news in recent years. This has turned Jordan into a popular destination for short-term mission teams, a change from the past. Some local churches find themselves hosting teams nonstop from January to December. Multiple teams from different countries often arrive simultaneously and leave the local church in a flurry of activity to host them.

In one church I visited recently, four foreign teams were present at the same time. Often there is little coordination between them and no continuity of work from one team to another. Nor does the local church benefit from these visits in any manner. This surplus of short-termers symbolizes the challenge of sharing resources when some donor nations are so much more wealthy and powerful than are the recipient communities. Without careful planning, well-intentioned giving may backfire, betraying donors and harming recipients.

For a few local churches involved in outreach to Syrian refugees, relying on foreign partners has become trendy. Jordanian evangelical congregations are small; one hundred members is considered a large church. Yet the refugees' need is greater. Thus it is natural for a local church to enter into an international partnership when one is offered. Such partnerships follow a similar pattern. In the beginning, the church may develop simple charity projects as a platform for serving refugees. Before long, their ministry attracts foreign churches, missionaries, and short-term teams who bring resources to partner with them. As time passes, the local church receives more and more foreign funds to start new projects, which attracts more partners and donors, and so on.

Although this kind of partnership seems to benefit both sides—the local churches provide platforms for foreign churches and field workers, and the foreign partners are helpful in "linking social capital"[10] to attract refugees— there are also some potential problems.

Due to an authoritarian leadership style and top-down church structure in Jordan, the pastor usually is at the center of all ministries. All resources and partnerships are channeled through the pastor. He controls the networks and access to finances. Unlike NGOs or faith-based ministry organizations, a church often does not have a board to oversee expenses, nor do they receive financial reports. In some cases, the pastor is the only person handling all financial matters. Overall, there is a lack of transparency and accountability in the handling of money in some churches and ministries involved with refugees.

Churches involved in Syrian refugee ministry, and in some cases Iraqi refugee ministry, often receive large amounts of foreign funds in regular installments to carry out projects such as medical services, renting or buying school buildings, and relief distribution. Some adopt the practice common among NGOs and faith-based organizations of taking 10–15 percent of donations as an administration fee. This money goes to the church account. Although the pastor may have a pure heart and no intent to steal, he may lack money-management skills, or time to oversee project administration, or even simple good judgment. Donors should find this structure problematic.

On the other hand, recipients can be overwhelmed by powerful donors. For example, projects requested by foreigners can dominate the ministry priorities of the local church. If donors would like to bring a short-term team to conduct a summer camp, the pastor will reorganize everything in the ministry around that event. While he is busy connecting with partners, starting new projects, and hosting short-term mission teams sent by partners, the pastor is distracted from ministry, as he functions more like a director of an NGO than a shepherd.

---

10 Robert J. Priest, "Short-term Mission as a New Paradigm," in *Mission after Christendom: Emergent Themes in Contemporary Mission*, ed. Ogbu Kalu, Peter Vethanayagamony, and Edmund Kee-Fook Chia (Louisville, KY: Westminster John Knox, 2010), 84–99.

Even though this kind of refugee ministry is a channel for the goodwill of the foreign body of Christ and allows them to serve and help Syrian refugees, this type of partnership may not build up the local body of Christ long-term. As Jonathon Bonk said in *Mission and Money*, "Affluence-dependent strategies cannot and should not be imitated by those whom Western missionaries presume to instruct."[11]

In such circumstances—when the need is great, the power difference is great, and the local expertise is limited—perhaps other models can be found. On one occasion, an American church desired to build a playground for a church-owned school serving Syrian refugees. The school wanted the playground. Instead of giving money directly to the local church, however, the donor gave the money to a faith-based NGO, which then built the playground and presented it to the church as a gift. This approach fulfills the principle, "It is usually best not to channel such a large amount of money to small churches or to individuals, but to organizations that have demonstrated track records of long-run, developmental ministry with strong financial and managerial accountability systems."[12]

CONCLUSION

The gratefulness of an Iraqi refugee in Jordan made me realize what God is doing amid the refugee crisis: "I thank God, and I thank this church, and I even thank ISIS because they pushed us out into the journey that led us to Jesus the Lord."

Such remarkable testimonies about God working among scattered people are heard again and again. In the middle of the suffering of refugees in the Middle East, God is doing some amazing things. When we look at history all the way back to the book of Acts, we see that God works in special ways to advance his kingdom through diasporas, or the movement of peoples to foreign places. I pray for more testimonies out of the contemporary diasporas, not only from Iraqis, but also from Syrians and Yemenis.

There is no doubt that God is active in the Middle East amid the greatest humanitarian crisis of our times. Yet even as we do his work, we will need insight from our Lord in order to carry it out in ways that please him. "Unless the Lord builds the house, the builders labor in vain" (Ps 127:1). May the Lord teach us to rely on divine love and wisdom, not our own strength and resources, to build up his kingdom.

---

11 Jonathan J. Bonk, *Mission and Money* (Maryknoll, NY: Orbis Books, 2006).

12 Steve Corbett and Brain Fikkert, *When Helping Hurts: How to Alleviate Poverty without Hurting the Poor . . . and Yourself* (Chicago: Moody, 2012).

chapter five

Somali Refugees and Friendly Churches

PETER M. SENSENIG, PhD

In 2016, Somali refugees to the United States were surpassed in number only by the Congolese. The recent travel ban threatens to strand thousands more Somali refugees. As one of the seven nations targeted by the ban, Somalia represents a complex and tragic history of Western involvement and an ongoing humanitarian puzzle. Simplistic responses like the current travel ban threaten to undermine one of the most compelling mission opportunities for the church in the West. At the same time, the experience of Mennonite congregations in the US receiving Somali refugees can provide insight into the challenges and opportunities for mission.

WHO IS COMING AND WHY?

According to the US State Department, approximately one hundred thousand Somali refugees settled in the United States between 2000 and 2016. An overwhelming majority were Muslims (99.7 percent), and most were young (more than three quarters under thirty-one years old and more than half under twenty-one years old). Most also had little formal education, with 91 percent completing primary school or less and only 1 percent with some kind of tertiary degree.[1]

---

1   State Department Bureau of Population, Refugees and Migration's Refugee Processing Center, available at the Center for Immigration Studies website, https://cis.org/Rush/Somali-Refugees-US (accessed December 20, 2017).

The top three resettlement states are Minnesota, Texas, and Ohio. Minnesota has long been a hub for Somali immigration, beginning with the hiring of Somalis to work in poultry plants in 1992. The famous Somali news chain attracts new refugees to the places that gain a reputation for economic opportunity—and where Somali pioneers have already forged a way.[2]

The push factors driving an entire generation of Somalis from their homeland are familiar to many. Civil war deposed the dictator Mohamed Siad Barre in 1991, and competing warlords threw the country into chaos. A devastating famine and ill-fated foreign military interventions displaced many thousands of Somalis in the early 1990s, and political instability ever since has facilitated waves of Somali migration to the West. Another push factor is the marginalization of Somali Bantus by the clan-based Somalis.[3] Political or religious issues can threaten the lives of such second-class citizens, making them refugees even in the absence of open civil war.

The pull factors drawing Somalis to the US are not only the promise of political freedom and stability, but also the economic opportunities. The expectations of immigrants are often checked by the harsh realities upon arrival. At the same time, many Somali refugees do find a better life in the US: running successful businesses, getting a good education, and even remitting money to family members in the Horn of Africa.

WHAT ARE THE CHALLENGES?

The pull factors of freedom and opportunities set refugees up to experience a cycle of four general stages. The exciting dreams of a good life (stage 1) give way to the reality of adjustment (stage 2), followed by culture shock that can produce depression and anxiety (stage 3). Many refugees finally find ways to cope and accept their new life (stage 4), but they can also be thrown back into other stages at different points in their journey.[4]

Most Somali refugees land in economically disadvantaged neighborhoods in urban centers. It is in this context that the harsh reality and the culture shock set it. Without proficiency in English, refugees fall prey to unscrupulous landlords, cultural misunderstandings in schools and communities, and missed medical and social service appointments. In the words of a man named Abdi, "I became frightened for [Somali refugees] . . . because, if I, though one of the luckiest few

---

2 Ahmed I. Yusuf, *Somalis in Minnesota* (St. Paul, MN: Minnesota Historical Society, 2012), Kindle edition.

3 Sandra M. Chait, *Seeking Salaam: Ethiopians, Eritreans, and Somalis in the Pacific Northwest* (Seattle: University of Washington Press, 2011), Kindle edition, 22.

4 D. L. Mayfield, "Preface: Stateless Wanderers," in *Assimilate or Go Home: Notes from a Failed Missionary on Rediscovering Faith* (New York: HarperCollins, 2016), Kindle edition, location 79.

with a college degree and a good command of the English language, was fighting with my own demons of doubt, how would a single mother . . . of six or more with neither the educational background nor employable skills, survive?"[5]

HOW ARE CHURCHES RESPONDING?

For some Somali refugees, the answer to Abdi's question, "How will they survive?" has been the hospitality of churches. Refugee resettlement agencies work hard to meet the needs of newly arrived Somalis and others. But they observe a huge difference in the rate of successful acclimation between families that have a church to sponsor them and families that do not. Without a church sponsor, refugee families often miss appointments, find it harder to get employment, and are more likely to move on to another location.

Churches that receive refugees can observe all of these stages of adjustment. One of the Mennonite churches that sponsored a Muslim Somali family in Pennsylvania noted that their arrival was characterized by excitement about getting a car, a well-paying job, and a fulfilling education. Then the weather, a car accident without a driving license, unknown foods, strange medical systems, ideas about time management, and—most importantly—language barriers hit them hard, and the family almost fell apart. One daughter ran away, and stories of the trauma they had experienced in the refugee camps began to surface. Another Somali refugee commented that without the sponsorship of the church, the family surely would have tried to start all over again somewhere else. By his account, because the congregation was "with them 100 percent, they said to me, 'We cannot believe that Christians did this for us.'"[6] Eventually, the family began to find ways to cope with their new life in spite of all these challenges.

Another Mennonite church in Pennsylvania had ties to Somalia through Mennonite missionaries who had served there before the civil war. So they offered to sponsor a Somali refugee family through the local resettlement agency. The church formed a welcoming team that was well prepared when the family of four arrived in December 2012. The team found a house and furnished it with help from the congregation, paying the family's rent for a year out of a special line in the church budget. They set up a schedule to drive the family to appointments and made school arrangements for the children. Whenever household items were needed, church members quickly responded, and one person even donated a small car. One member of the welcoming team stated, "We were on 24-7 call if there was a problem."[7]

5 Yusuf, *Somalis in Minnesota*, locations 365–68.
6 Daoud Hersi (pseudonym), Skype interview by author, September 25, 2016.
7 I. L. and M. E. L. (Springfield Welcoming Team), Skype interview by author, October 9, 2016.

Unlike many Somalis, this particular family was Christian, and as a result they were able to plug directly into congregational life, attending Sunday services and church events and participating in monthly gatherings to pray for Somalia. They found the church and the pastoral leadership to be warmly intentional about fostering diversity, and the relationship has developed into a dynamic of mutuality.[8]

While the church provided a wide range of logistical help, from driving lessons to a teen mentoring program, the Somali family has been an important part of congregational revitalization. In the words of the father of the family, "Many people did not know about Somalis or had negative views, but now they have learned from us who Somalis are. And they are now awaiting any Somali family; they keep asking me if I know anyone who is coming."[9]

Before long, he developed a thriving ministry to newly arrived Somali refugees. He states, "I felt the Holy Spirit guiding me to be helpful, because the way that I experienced being a refugee, I knew others would have the same experience. I saw Somali families are struggling. It's informal, but [the agency] calls me to help with particular families."[10]

Reminiscent of Jesus' yeast metaphor in Matthew 13:33, one church's welcoming of a Somali refugee family has in turn impacted both the local community and individuals around the world.

HOW SHOULD WE RESPOND?

Our response to the realities driving Somali refugees to our home communities, and to refugees in general, should be shaped by three basic principles.

First, *Christian hospitality toward refugees comes with practice*. Communities that have successfully resettled one refugee group are better equipped to assist other groups. For example, Minneapolis resettled Southeast Asian refugees in the 1970s, which enabled them to set up the social services later for Somali refugees.[11][29] The same is true for churches; once a congregation has become attuned to the specific needs of new arrivals, the DNA of the community changes irreversibly. A church that receives refugees will not experience it as a one-time endeavor, but rather becomes a kind of community that practices such hospitality. In both of the Mennonite churches mentioned in this chapter, receiving refugees was a habitual practice; and they even developed a reputation

---

8 Ibid.
9 Hersi interview.
10 Ibid.
11 Yusuf, *Somalis in Minnesota*, location 694.

with the resettlement agencies as a community that knew how to value diversity and to help newcomers acclimate to their new life.

Second, *interfaith interactions are healthy for Christian individuals and communities.* One Somali Christian who helps other Somali refugees adjust to life in the US is often privy to the ways that deeply held assumptions are challenged. He observes, "Muslim families have told me, what we believed before was that Christians are our enemies. But when we came to the US that idea was washed out; now we know that they are not enemies but are helpful to us." For some Somali Muslims, interacting with Christians is a stretch, let alone setting foot in a church. Yet in spite of this barrier, he has Muslim friends who join him on occasion in attending church services.[12]

Another surprising result of interfaith encounters is that given identity markers can be challenged. The Mennonite history in Somalia provides some interesting examples. The precarious Mennonite presence of education and health work in Somalia continued through national independence, war, dictatorship, famine, martyrdom, and nationalization of the Mennonite schools. But over time a remarkable rapport was built that lasts to the present day. In Toronto, Atlanta, or Hargeisa one meets Somalis who studied in the Mennonite schools and speak affectionately of their Mennonite teachers, and even some who refer to themselves as Mennonite Muslims.[13] What this means is that they have embraced the identity of peacemaking that transcends clan division, which they saw reflected in Mennonite theology and practice.

Part of the tragedy of the travel ban targeting arrivals from majority-Muslim nations is that it will make such interfaith encounters more difficult and less likely. The response of Christians should be to seek out those of other faiths in friendship, attempting to share our lives rather than to create a society free of the other.

Third, *receiving refugees is central to the mission of the church.* It is second nature for many churches to imagine mission with Somalis along the traditional lines of sending missionaries to a majority-Somali context. In fact, churches and mission organizations prove willing to invest huge amounts of training, personnel, and financial resources within the sending paradigm. What is more difficult is to embrace the reality that an equally important missional approach is to welcome the Somalis who are coming to the doorsteps of these same churches, often with deep needs for assistance, friendship, and mutual sharing.

---

12 Hersi interview.

13 Peter M. Sensenig, *Peace Clan: Mennonite Peacemaking in Somalia* (Eugene, OR: Wipf and Stock/ Pickwick, 2016), xxi.

When our family moved to Somaliland to begin an assignment with Mennonite Board, people in our sending congregations sometimes asked us what they could do to help. Our response was always this: Simply make friends with the Somalis who are in your hometown, either as newly arrived refugees or as a more established community. The Somali grapevine is so effective that our neighbors in Hargeisa are likely acquainted with your Somali neighbors in the US.

In short, the way we treat refugees matters: for mission at home and abroad, for the sake of obedience to Jesus the refugee, and for the goal of a better world. We close with the words of one Somali refugee: "Let churches follow the way Jesus said himself: to receive those who are new, to not discriminate."[14]

---

14 Hersi interview.

chapter six

Iraq: What Happened to the Christians?

DR. WISSAM PAULUS KAMMOU

By the end of 2017, over three-fourths of Iraq's Christians had fled their hometowns. The ongoing war and escalating persecution at the hand of tyrants and radical Islamists over decades have scattered Iraqis all over the Middle East, Europe, North America, and elsewhere. While some have found shelter abroad, others fled their homes to become "internally displaced people" within Iraq or are languishing in refugee camps hoping to escape to a more secure place soon. This chapter underscores, from an insider perspective, some factors behind this large-scale displacement of Iraqi people.

CHRISTIANITY IN IRAQ

According to historians, the apostles Thomas and Bartholomew preached the gospel to the Assyrians of Iraq soon after Jesus was resurrected, and Assyria became one of the first nations to convert to Christianity. Assyrians have inhabited their homeland of the Nineveh Plains, a swath of fertile land in northern Iraq surrounding Mosul (Nineveh), for more than five thousand years. The Assyrian (also known as Syriac and Chaldean) Christians descended from the same Ninevites who repented when they heard Jonah's message. When Iraqis heard the gospel from the apostles, many believed; and numerous churches and monasteries appeared all across the land. They sent out many pastors and missionaries to neighboring regions and to lands as far away as India. When Muslims gained power, however, Christians were forced either to embrace Islam, pay heavy taxes (*jizya*), or die. Persecution varied in intensity, depending on which Islamic group ruled the land in each successive period of Iraq's history, and the legacy of an unbroken Christian presence since the first century is at risk of disappearing altogether.

Iraq became an independent country in 1921, and since then many different forms of government have ruled the country with a mixture of liberal and Islamic political ideology. But it always included a reasonable proportion of Christian, Jewish, and Yezidi minority representatives, which helped maintain relative peace and harmony between the diverse communities of Iraq. As per the last official census in 1987, there were 1.4 million Christians in Iraq, although the number dwindled to around 1 million after the fall of Saddam Hussein in 2003. That number has continued to decline as more Christians have fled the land. It is difficult to obtain the latest figures of religious adherence in Iraq, but some estimate that less than 200,000 Christians are left in Iraq now, since so many have been forcefully displaced from their homes.

The attacks on Iraqi Christians did not begin in 2014 when ISIS took over large areas of land. Iraqi Christians' mass flight began over a decade earlier, in 2003. The ongoing sectarian conflict, which exploded during the US-led conflict, strengthened the militant Islamic insurgent groups; and as a result, persecution against Christians skyrocketed. It is estimated that over two-thirds of the Iraqi Christian population fled their homes between 2003 and 2011 to seek shelter elsewhere. Most Iraqi Christians now live in Kurdish-controlled areas, who arrived as displaced people from Arab areas as a result of targeted attacks, torture, and violence at the hands of Al-Qaeda or ISIS.

War had been oozing over Iraq for two decades. During the first Gulf War (1980–88) the number of Christians remained stable, but after the second Gulf War (1990–91), and especially during the economic embargo that lasted twelve years until 2003, many waves of large-scale migration began. Many Christians, including my parents and siblings, left for Jordan and subsequently the United States. I stayed in Iraq with my wife and children to serve my people and because of my ministry responsibilities. After the collapse of Saddam Hussein's regime and the subsequent American-led military operation, more Christians fled to wherever they could live in peace and make a living to support their families. In some places they received a warm welcome from active churches and ministries, but in other places they suffered much.

When the Islamic State spread across much of Iraq between 2014 and 2017, more Christians—especially from Mosul, Qaraqosh, and the Nineveh Plains— left for countries like Lebanon and Turkey. Many from Qaraqosh, which was considered the largest Catholic community in the Middle East, were forcefully displaced. They immigrated to the West by passing through nearby countries to secure refugee documentation from United Nations representatives.

In spite of numerous tragedies accompanying these waves of forced migration and religious persecution, a shining light amid the darkness is that many displaced people have come to know Jesus through dramatic encounters and have accepted him as their Lord and Savior. They are being discipled and trained, and many serve actively as church members, leaders, and pastors in their landed destinations in the West. Another exciting fact is that a few have returned to Iraq to serve existing churches or to begin new churches and ministries reaching out to those who remain.

Figure 6: Major Refugee-producing Nations of the World (2006–16)

2006	Afghanistan	Iraq	Sudan	2012	Afghanistan	Somalia	Iraq
2007	Afghanistan	Iraq	Colombia	2013	Afghanistan	Syria	Somalia
2008	Afghanistan	Iraq	Somalia	2014	Syria	Afghanistan	Somalia
2009	Afghanistan	Iraq	Somalia	2015	Syria	Afghanistan	Somalia
2010	Afghanistan	Iraq	Somalia	2016	Syria	Afghanistan	South Sudan
2011	Afghanistan	Iraq	Somalia				

MURDER OF AN ARCHBISHOP

Paul Faraj Rahho was born into a Chaldean Catholic family in 1942 and spent nearly all of his life in Mosul, a city with one of the largest and oldest Christian populations in Iraq. After studying at St. Peter's Seminary in Baghdad, he was ordained and appointed to St. Isiah's Church in Mosul. Between 1974 and 1976, Rahho studied at the Pontifical University of Saint Thomas Aquinas in Rome. He founded the Church of the Sacred Heart in Tel Keppe (which is my parents' hometown), twelve miles north of Mosul, and also opened an orphanage for handicapped children.

On January 12, 2001, the synod of bishops of the Chaldean Catholic Church elected Rahho archbishop of Mosul; and he was ordained by the patriarch of Babylon to serve as the Chaldean archbishop, giving him responsibility for around twenty thousand Catholics in ten parishes. His church was known in Mosul as Safina (The Ship), but parishioners called it the Holy Spirit Church.

Archbishop Rahho refused to settle into a comfortable liturgical routine, but instead spoke up for his people. Specifically, he protested the moves to incorporate sharia law into the Iraqi constitution. Following the start of the Iraq war, when persecution increased dramatically, Rahho commented on the precarious situation of Chaldean Christians in an interview with AsiaNews, and he continued to lead worship in very difficult circumstances. When he visited Rome in 2007 with former patriarch of Babylon Emmanuel III Delly, who was then appointed as cardinal, Rahho confided that he had been threatened by gunmen in his hometown.

According to the Catholic News Service on February 29, 2008, Rahho was kidnapped from his car in the Al-Nur district of the city of Mosul. The captors sprayed bullets on the archbishop's car, killed two bodyguards, and shoved Rahho into the trunk of a car. In the darkness, Rahho managed to pull out his cellphone and call the church, telling officials not to pay a ransom for his release. He believed the money would be used for killing and evil activities. The kidnappers demanded a ransom of $3 million for Rahho's release and asked Christians to contribute to the jihad by paying the special *jizya* tax. They also demanded the release of non-Iraqi Arab detainees and the formation of an Iraqi Christian militia to fight against the US forces.

Later, church officials received a call informing them of the archbishop's body being found in a shallow grave near the city, but reports of the cause of death remain contradictory. Since police reported that "his body bore no bullet wounds," and Rahho had high blood pressure and diabetes, he might have died from natural causes. But when relatives and authorities went to the burial site, they reported that the body had many "gunshot wounds."

The identity of the killers remains equally disputed. Some in the Christian community believe Al-Qaida and other Sunni Arab factions were responsible. Other Christians, including the archbishop's family, believe that Kurds ordered his assassination. Kurdish authorities investigated and made several arrests, but their reports have failed to convince the family.

Archbishop Rahho is believed to be the highest-ranking Chaldean Catholic clergyman to have been killed in the Iraq war. Ahmed Ali Ahmed, who had led an Al-Qaida cell in Mosul, was arrested; and the Iraqi Central Criminal Court sentenced him to death. However, the representatives of the Chaldean Catholic Church opposed the death sentence. In his will, Rahho called upon the Iraqi Assyrian Christian community to work with Muslim and Yezidi Iraqis to develop ties across religious divisions within the nation.

MASSACRES AND ATTACKS

Protestants also came under severe persecution in Iraq. For example, consider the tragedy of Pastor Haytham Halawi. Although he was born in Iraq, Halawi studied and was ordained in Beirut, Lebanon. He returned to Iraq in 2004 and started the Mosul Baptist Church in the Al-Masarif neighborhood of the city. While he and his mother were ministering in the Assyrian town of Bartial in November of 2004, they were suddenly attacked by gunmen. Pastor Halawi suffered spinal cord injuries that left him partially paralyzed. Some friends helped him escape across the border to Syria, and from there he traveled to Lebanon. Today he is pastor of Christ Bible Baptist Church in the Jal al Dib neighborhood near Beirut.

Not only have individuals like Archbishop Rahho and Pastor Halawi been targeted, but also entire churches. The first major attack against Christians after the 2003 invasion was a series of six car bombs. In August of 2004, assassins struck churches in Baghdad and Mosul during Sunday services. Cars parked outside the buildings were rigged with explosives; as parishioners began to leave, the explosives detonated—killing twelve people and wounding seventy-one. A previously unknown group from Pakistan claimed responsibility for the attack on an Islamic website.

In October of 2010, six suicide jihadis from the Islamic State of Iraq attacked a Syrian Catholic Church in Baghdad during Sunday evening mass. About one hundred worshipers were herded to the center of the church; the gunmen turned off the lights and began shooting. Rev. Thaer Abdal was killed at the altar. According to one witness, the gunmen, who were just youths, claimed they were avenging "the burning of the Qur'an and the jailing of Muslim women in Egypt." They phoned the television station Al-Baghdadia to claim the attack and demanded the release of al-Qaeda prisoners held by the Coptic Church in Egypt. The Islamic State of Iraq was a Sunni militant umbrella group to which Al-Qaeda in Iraq belonged to. When Iraqi security forces stormed the church grounds late in the evening, the gunmen threatened to kill all the hostages. As US forces provided air support, Iraqi forces blew open the church doors and rushed inside, but the gunmen opened fire on the hostages, causing mass slaughter. In the church basement a gunman killed thirty more hostages with grenades with the explosive vest he was wearing.

ISI posted an audio message on a jihadist website claiming responsibility for the attack and calling for the release of two Egyptian female Muslims, whom they alleged were being held against their will in Coptic Christian monasteries in Egypt. They called the church "the dirty den of idolatry"; and since the women had not been freed, the fuse of a campaign against Iraqi Christians had been lit. They declared

> all Christian centers, organizations and institutions, leaders and followers to
> be legitimate targets for the *mujahedeen* wherever they can reach them. Let these
> idolaters, and the hallucinating tyrant of the Vatican, know that the killing

sword will not be lifted from the necks of their followers until they declare their innocence from what the dog of the Egyptian Church is doing . . . [and] pressure this belligerent church to release the captive women from the prisons of their monasteries.

DESTRUCTION BY ISIS

When the US invaded Iraq in 2003, it instituted a "de-Ba'athification" program that terminated members of Saddam Hussein's Ba'ath Party from employment and access to pensions. Al-Qaeda capitalized on the anger of disenfranchised Sunnis who were marginalized through this program, and the destabilizing effect of the ongoing civil war in Syria resulted in ISIS becoming stronger. It is important to note that ISIS was born not only from religious fanaticism and the US invasion of Iraq, but from intersecting factors such as the rise of sectarianism across the Middle East, repressive governments, proxy interests of outside regional and international leaders, and power vacuums left behind from internal conflicts—including the struggles of the Arab Spring.

After capturing the cities of Raqqa and Deir ez-Zor in Syria, ISIS conducted a lightning offensive into Iraq in the summer of 2014, taking Mosul in the north, Ramadi and Fallujah in the east, and driving south almost to Baghdad. ISIS spread its self-styled caliphate from Turkey's border across Syria and as far as Fallujah in Iraq, encompassing an area roughly the size of the state of Indiana in the United States. After Mosul fell, ISIS required Iraqi Christians to convert to Islam, pay tribute, or face execution. Christians who did not agree with those terms by the deadline of July 19, 2014, must "leave the borders of the Islamic Caliphate." On Christians' homes, the militants painted a red Arabic " ن = n" for *Nasrani*, a slur referring to Christians. These acts precipitated the further exodus of Christians from Mosul, ending over 1,900 years of Christian presence there.

By August, ISIS had captured the Assyrian towns of Qaraqosh, Tel Keppe, Bartella, and Karamlish in the Nineveh Plains. Approximately one hundred thousand Iraqi Christians were forced to flee their homes and leave behind all their property, including currency and gold. Many were left with only the clothes on their backs and were forced to live with extended family or in construction sites, parking structures, churches, unwinterized tents, and parks—with little access to food, water, sanitation, or medical care. Many Christians carried with them tales of executions, crucifixions, beheadings, kidnappings, forced conversions, and seizure of homes and property. Christian families were separated from each other, children were taken away from parents, and young girls and women were raped and forced into the ISIS sex trade, along with many Yezidi women.

Beyond persecution, ISIS made a systematic effort to destroy the cultural heritage of ancient communities, including the destruction of Christian churches, monasteries, and the tombs of prophets and the desecration of cemeteries and ancient artifacts. St. Elijah monastery, which stood for more than 1,400 years above a riverbed south of Mosul, was razed to the ground. The campaign of genocide and destruction of all Christian history and identity in Iraq, the fighters ransacked the Mosul Museum—destroying centuries-old manuscripts and the library, bulldozed the ancient Assyrian city of Nimrud, and demolished parts of the 2000-year-old UNESCO World Heritage city of Hatra. The destruction of Nimrud, a 3300-year-old Assyrian site, has been called a "war crime." US Secretary of State John Kerry declared that ISIS was responsible for genocide against minority groups, including Yezidis, Christians, and Shia Muslims.

CONCLUSION

It is evident from the accounts above that a large number of Iraqi Christians were forced to flee their homelands as part of a campaign to kill Iraqi Christian leaders, attack churches, and systematically destroy ancient Christian heritage sites in the land. The fleeing Iraqi Christians end up waiting from two to five years in refugee camps before they are allowed to enter Western countries. The inadequate resources, unsanitary living conditions, and lack of medical care make life difficult in the refugee camps. Many have perished while fleeing or while living in refugee camps. Some Iraqis decide to go back and adapt to the unstable security situation and political mess in their ancestral homeland. Moreover, it is possible that a new wave of forced refugee displacement of Christians may result from the recent conflicts between the Kurdish people and the Iraqi central government.

chapter seven

Refugee Ministries in East Africa

KEVIN PANICKER

Imagine that the government which is meant to protect you and your family decides that you are its enemy—for no other reason than because of your ethnic background. You have no weapons and no intention of rebellion, but because of your ethnicity soldiers attack your home or community, indiscriminately killing all within sight. You watch as women are raped and killed in front of their families. Children are tied to the bodies of their dead mothers and thrown into the river. Your home is burned down and you are forced to run for your life, carrying nothing with you—no food, no water, no belongings.

These horrific scenes are the reality for many people who have fled South Sudan for their lives, thereby having to own the unenviable status of "refugees."

Contrary to media depictions and popular belief, most refugees from the Middle East and Africa are not fleeing to Europe or America, but are being hosted by neighboring countries. According to the latest UNCHR figures (as of June 2017), 55 percent of refugees worldwide come from three countries: Syria (5.5 million), Afghanistan (2.5 million), and South Sudan (1.4 million), while the top three refugee-hosting countries are Turkey (2.9 million), Pakistan (1.4 million), and Lebanon (1 million). It is estimated that more people sought refuge in Uganda in 2016 than those who crossed the Mediterranean on their way to Europe. More than a quarter of the world's refugee population is hosted in sub-Saharan Africa, with Kenya accommodating one of the largest refugee camps in the world. This chapter addresses the three largest refugee situations in East Africa—namely South Sudanese refugees in Uganda and Kenya, and Somali refugees in Kenya.

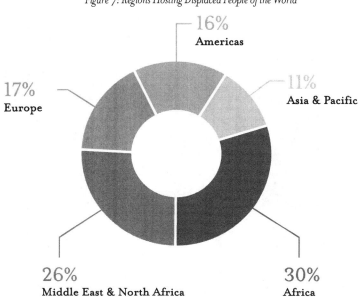

Figure 7: Regions Hosting Displaced People of the World

16%
Americas

11%
Asia & Pacific

17%
Europe

26%
Middle East & North Africa

30%
Africa

Source: UNHCR/June 2017

REFUGEE SITUATIONS IN EAST AFRICA

According to the 2017 annual report of the UNHCR, East Africa hosts the largest number of displaced people in the world—over 10 million individuals, of whom 3.3 million are refugees. This region has been host to one of the longest-running refugee situations in modern history—that of Somali refugees, which lasted for more than a quarter of a century. The East African countries hosting the most refugees are Uganda, Ethiopia, and Kenya, while the countries from which the largest number of people are fleeing are South Sudan, Somalia, and Eritrea.

For decades, people from South Sudan have sought refuge in neighboring Uganda and Kenya, which have been relatively stable and have had open policies toward refugees. The first movements occurred soon after Sudan's independence in 1956, during the first civil war in Sudan. These movements subsided following a 1972 peace agreement, but the second civil war started in 1983 and didn't end until twenty-two years later, with another peace pact in 2005.[1] Many returned to their homes, and in 2011 the people celebrated independence from Sudan and the creation of their own country.[2]

In late 2013, however, the new country descended into an ongoing civil war that has led once again to the movement of people into neighboring countries.[3] Many of these people fled to Uganda, which, by the middle of 2017, had earned the title of the most refugee-friendly country in the world for its very generous and welcoming posture to refugees. Over a million South Sudanese, 85 percent of whom are women and children, have sought safety in Uganda.

For years, Somalis fleeing their country have sought refuge in Kenya due to its geographic proximity and welcoming refugee policies. Before March of 1991, there were approximately 30,000 Somali refugees in Kenya; this number rapidly increased to 300,000 following the collapse of the state in Somalia.[4] Somali refugees arrived again following the drought and famine of 2011, during which the Dadaab refugee center reached its peak population of 485,000.[5] The menace of terrorist groups, such as Al-Shabaab, has worsened the situation, wreaking violence on the country and forcing even more to run for their lives. Many Somali refugees have remained in Kenya, as Somalia has not yet achieved needed security or stable conditions conducive for a return of refugees. With drought again in 2017, and the possibility of famine,[6] it is likely that even more Somali refugees will seek refuge in Kenya.

The massive increase in refugees comes at a time when resources are increasingly limited, as they must be stretched across multiple crises globally. This decrease in resources is felt by refugees in the most real way—in their stomachs. In refugee sites across East Africa, food rations have been reduced, in some cases by 75 percent. Unfortunately, the situations causing people to flee their homes appear to have no end in sight, so the displacement and suffering is only expected to increase and worsen. In circumstances where there are insufficient resources and capacity to provide for refugees, government agencies invite UNHCR to provide assistance, which in turn engages with foreign governments and other donors to solicit needed funds and engages in partnerships with various types of organizations to provide services directly to refugees.

---

1 Conflict in South Sudan: Refugees Seek Protection in Uganda and a Way Home (International Refugee Rights Initiative, 2014).

2 Matthew Arnold and Matthew LeRiche, *South Sudan: From Revolution to Independence* (New York: Oxford University Press, 2013).

3 "UN: Refugees from South Sudan Cross 1.5 Million Mark," Al Jazeera, http://www.aljazeera.com/news/2017/02/number-refugees-south-sudan-crosses-15m-170210101935179.html (accessed March 3, 2017).

4 Laura Hammond, *History, Overview, Trends and Issues in Major Somali Refugee Displacements in the near Region*, Issues in Refugee Research (Geneva: UNHCR Policy Development and Evaluation Service, 2014).

5 *Somalia Situation Supplementary Appeal* (United Nations High Commission for Refugees, 2016).

6 "Somalia: Operational Plan for Famine Prevention (Jan–Jun 2017)," UN Office for the Coordination of Humanitarian Affairs, 2017.

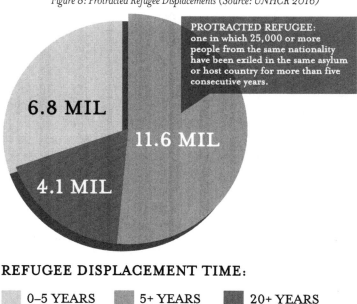

Figure 8: Protracted Refugee Displacements (Source: UNHCR 2016)

PROTRACTED REFUGEE:
one in which 25,000 or more
people from the same nationality
have been exiled in the same asylum
or host country for more than five
consecutive years.

6.8 MIL

11.6 MIL

4.1 MIL

REFUGEE DISPLACEMENT TIME:

0–5 YEARS   5+ YEARS   20+ YEARS

REFUGEE MINISTRIES IN EAST AFRICA

The majority of South Sudanese refugees arriving in Uganda identify themselves as Christian, while others identify as Muslim or adherents of traditional African religions. There are a large number of Christian organizations and missionaries working or seeking to work among refugees in these camps. Christian entities responding to the refugee crisis include churches, parachurch organizations, foreign missionaries, and faith-based NGOs. South Sudanese refugees generally welcome Christian ministries and missionaries, and the risk of persecution or attack on such missionaries is relatively low.[7]

The churches of South Sudan have been heavily involved in ministering to the needs of refugees. As the scale of displacement has been massive, church leaders have in essence followed their flock to Uganda. South Sudanese churches have partnered with Ugandan churches, which have enabled them to operate legally and minister to refugees. One example of such a partnership is that of the Episcopal Church of South Sudan and Sudan (ECS), which has worked with the (Anglican) Church of Uganda. Their ministry has involved organizing prayers and worship services for refugees; preaching the Word; and providing

---

7 Interview with Bishop B. J. B., March 21, 2017.

relief supplies, psychosocial services, peace and reconciliation workshops, and advocacy with government and other agencies on behalf of refugees.

Churches seek to meet refugees as they arrive and provide them with immediate relief materials, along with encouragement and messages of hope in the midst of suffering and loneliness. Church and lay leaders are being identified among refugees and encouraged to lead congregations within the camps. In some cases, there is only one ordained minister for populations of up to six thousand.[8]

South Sudanese churches have been encouraging local Ugandan churches to reach out to arriving refugees, and in many cases Ugandan churches have gathered donations for refugees and sent volunteers to the camps. Widespread prayer is reported among Ugandan churches on behalf of the arriving refugees.[9] Apart from the Episcopal/Anglican Church, other churches reportedly involved include those identifying as Adventist, Africa Inland Church, Baptist, Charismatic, Church of Christ, Healing Church, Presbyterian, Roman Catholic, Sudanese Pentecostal, and World Harvest Church.

As with the churches, South Sudanese parachurch organizations are also involved in reaching out to refugees in Uganda, through partnerships with their counterparts in Uganda. Scripture Union of South Sudan and Uganda have partnered, for instance, to hold workshops and other activities within the camps. They have realized that while the work of the humanitarian agencies is reaching many people, there are major gaps—such as forgiveness and reconciliation between people and the need for refugees to be reassured of God's love for them. With donations from South Sudan and Uganda, three ministry camps were held to reach out to 1,863 children, youth, and pastors in December of 2016. These activities involved the mobilization of volunteers from among the refugees in the camps, along with a partnership with Biblica for the provision of Bibles and literature.[10]

Foreign missionaries and ministries have also reached out to South Sudanese refugees arriving in Uganda. Some of these are already established in Uganda, while others are or were based in South Sudan and are ministering in Uganda to the same people. Youth with a Mission (YWAM) has an established presence in Uganda and has made weekly visits to the camps to minister to refugees through trauma healing, prayer ministry, and discipleship. Pioneers has missionaries in Uganda who have volunteered at medical centers for refugees.[11] Harvesters Reaching the Nations, which has been running a school in South Sudan, followed people who fled to Uganda and has plans to open a school

---

8 Interview with missionaries K. K. and L. V., March 20, 2017.

9 Interview with national director D. Z. S., March 24, 2017.

10 Aloro Peter Satimon and Manse Woja Alfred, *Refugee Ministry in Uganda—Arua District* (Juba: Scripture Union of South Sudan, 2017).

11 Interview with missionary A. R., February 27, 2017.

for refugees.[12] Similarly, Development and Literacy Partners International (DLPI) has relocated its Bible translation activities to the camps in Uganda and has ministered through trauma healing, prayer, and children's ministries. Other mission organizations that are involved or seek to be involved in ministering to refugees are Africa Inland Mission (AIM) and the International Mission Board (IMB). E3 Partners, a US-based mission organization, intends to send several short-term ministry teams to Uganda to work with refugees.

Alongside churches and ministries are faith-affiliated foreign and local NGOs that are working in partnership with or independently of UNHCR. These include Across, Caritas, Danish Church Aid, Finn Church Aid, Food for the Hungry, Lutheran World Federation, Medical Teams International, Samaritan's Purse, Tutapona Trauma Rehabilitation, Water Mission Uganda, and the Dutch agency ZOA.

In Kenya, South Sudanese refugees in the Kakuma refugee camp identify themselves largely as Christians.[13] Ministry among South Sudanese refugees is greatly encouraged by Christian and missionary organizations in Kenya. Among the Christian entities reaching out to South Sudanese refugees are local churches and parachurch organizations, local and international NGOs, and missionaries. Local churches in Kenya have enabled South Sudanese congregations to operate in Kenya, both in regard to legal registration and the use of physical church facilities.[14]

Among the other organizations working among refugees in Kenya is the National Council of Churches of Kenya (NCCK). NCCK has had a longstanding partnership with UNHCR, and has provided various services in Kakuma, including school construction, health campaigns, services to elderly and disabled people, and supporting the livelihood activities of refugees so that they can support themselves.[15] Other organizations working with refugees in Kenya include Lutheran World Federation, World Vision, and Salesian-based Don Bosco Development Outreach Network, which focuses on vocational training for youth. Using curriculum developed by American Bible Society, Serving in Mission (SIM) carries out a ministry focused on trauma healing among refugees, and they have trained pastors and church leaders in trauma healing both for themselves and for their congregations.

The majority of Somali refugees arriving in Kenya are Muslim. While South Sudanese refugees may welcome Christian organizations and ministries to work among them, these Somali refugees prefer services provided by Islamic organizations. As in many Muslim countries, the conversion of a Somali from

12 Interview with J. M., on staff of Harvesters Reaching the Nations, February 27, 2017.
13 Interview with missionary D. D., March 20, 2017.
14 Interview with missionary T. G., March 22, 2017.
15 Interview with A. B., Programme Officer of the National Council of Churches in Kenya, March 24, 2017.

Islam to another religion is a life-threatening decision, with persecution and/ or death likely to follow. Among and around the refugee camps there also have been attacks by bandits and terrorist entities on refugees and humanitarian workers. In such places, any sort of work, much less ministry among refugees, is very difficult. Christian-affiliated organizations working in the Dadaab camp are the National Christian Council of Kenya (NCCK) and Lutheran World Federation. For over ten years NCCK has provided various services here, including shelter and HIV-related resources.[16]

Given the challenges of ministry in or around settlements of Somali refugees, some ministries have focused instead on reaching Somalis in areas where they have settled outside the camps. Some Somali refugees have become believers through the ministry of Kenyan churches, as well as through the work of other missionaries, and are being nurtured in their new faith.[17] For example, one missionary leads Bible studies with Somalis every week by inviting them to home gatherings. He recognizes the opportunity to minister to Somalis as a unique opening to reach people who come from unreached and closed countries.[18] Somali refugees in Kenya, especially in urban centers, generally are not welcomed, so they remain on the margins of society, with many living in abject poverty. There are many opportunities for Christians to demonstrate the love of Christ through ministries that address the medical, educational, and other needs of Somali refugees with practical means, such as English classes or trauma counseling.[19]

CONCLUSION

Those fleeing their home countries in East Africa are generally doing so not because of economic opportunity or to pursue a better life, but because they are running for life itself—away from a multiplicity of terrors: war, torture, rape, murder, hunger, and failing governments. These individuals are clearly in distress, and among them are many orphans and widows; being concerned about these people is one of the manifestations of "true religion" (James 1:27).

My involvement with the refugee situation in East Africa has helped me see how the church is indeed responding in many different ways through relief agencies, local churches, and missionaries. The most encouraging stories to me have been those involving local churches that with few resources, little publicity, and only basic training have embarked on a ministry of presence and compassion to refugees—and have done so because of their calling to be the body of Christ.

---

16 Interview with A. B., Programme Officer of the National Council of Churches in Kenya, March 24, 2017.

17 T. G., personal interview.

18 D. D., personal interview.

19 T. G., personal interview.

With increased awareness of the refugee crisis in our world, I hope some readers of this book will prayerfully consider what role they could play in ministering to refugees in this part of the world. For outsiders seeking to minister to the needs of those in refugee camps, it is important to secure the necessary approvals from governmental and local authorities. Given the background of ethnic conflict, it is extremely important that those working in these communities are sensitive to the issues surrounding conflict and reconciliation, so as not to inadvertently worsen tensions.

As refugees have little means to provide for themselves, but instead have to depend on others, it is important that we be sensitive regarding dependency. Having to subsist on handouts can have a harmful impact on a person's work ethic. How can churches and ministries serve refugees while at the same time discouraging a spirit of dependency? Among the ways recommended is to focus on spiritual discipleship.

Lastly, it is important to remember that people have had to flee largely due to political problems. Should the church be involved in advocating for change at this level?

chapter eight

Brazilian Ministries to Middle Eastern Refugees

José RM Prado

In 2013, when I was a pastor of a church in Sa̅o Paulo, I received a request to welcome a Syrian refugee family of eighteen people arriving in Brazil. This experience was so challenging and transformative that I later decided to leave local church ministry in order to dedicate myself entirely to ministering to refugees. Since then I have had the opportunity to develop and coordinate programs to support refugees in different ways, as well to participate in rescuing vulnerable refugee families who were arriving in São Paulo and other cities of Brazil.

In October 2015 my wife and I opened a shelter house for refugees, and in April 2016 we founded DIGNITÀ (meaning "dignity"), a nongovernmental organization that focuses on supporting refugees in Brazil. Since 2015 we have been involved with Refugee Highway Partnership, a global network of Christian refugee ministries, facilitating its activity for Brazil and Latin America. Thus a great part of my ministry has been dedicated to creating awareness and mobilizing Brazilian churches to minister to refugees.

REFUGEE SITUATION IN BRAZIL

It wasn't until 1982 that the Brazilian government officially recognized the UNHCR as a body of the United Nations. Between 1980 and 2000 Brazil gradually began to receive small groups of refugees. The number of applicants asking for refugee status rose exponentially between 2010 and 2015—from 966 applications in 2010 to 28,670 in 2015. Most are natives of Africa, Asia (taking into consideration the Middle East), and the Caribbean.

According to CONARE (National Committee for Refugees), around 93,000 people of ninety-five nationalities applied for refugee status in Brazil between 2010 and 2016. The number of applications decreased substantially (64 percent) between 2015 and 2016. Many factors explain this decrease, among them the worsening of the economic crisis in Brazil and the hardening of the politics of visa issuances to potential applicants. Of the total applicants, 49,000 (52.5 percent) are Haitians. The other 44,000 applicants are mainly from Senegal (7206), Venezuela (4904), Syria (3851), Angola (3634), Bangladesh (3445), Nigeria (2904), Congo (2549), and Ghana (2321).

In 2016, only 9552 refugee applications were approved out of which 68 percent of applicants were men and 32 percent were women. In terms of age, 41 percent were between eighteen and twenty-nine years old; and 47 percent were between thirty and fifty-nine years old. Due to political instability, some Venezuelans have recently crossed the border and applied for refugee status in Brazil. According to the federal police, 30,000 have crossed the northern border since 2016. When we compare the number of applicants asking for refugee status (93,000) to the Brazilian population (208 millions) we arrive at a proportion of less than 0.05 percent—which is, in fact, a very small percentage. If we take into consideration the number of received Syrians (3,851) from the total number of Syrians who are refugees in other nations (4.9 million), we reach a similar percentage (0.07 percent).

REFUGEE ENTRY ROUTES

For those who enter regularly with tourist visas by means of any Brazilian representation abroad, the main gateway is Guarulhos International Airport in São Paulo. Those who come from Africa and the Caribbean sometimes make a connection in Panama. Individuals who come from Asia and the Middle East make a connection in a country of the Gulf. Some arrive over land routes, mainly Haitians, Dominicans and Venezuelans, while Africans from countries such as Senegal and Sudan, and Asians from Bangladesh arrive by ships and planes. The most common border crossing is located in the state of Acre in Amazonia. This route is dangerous because it involves days of walking in the jungle and is exploited by "coyotes" (human traffickers). Others journey through Panama, then Quito, in Equator, then by bus to Lima in Peru, and eventually proceeding to the border crossing in Brasiléia. Then they proceed to Rio Branco, and after that they go to cities in the southern center and southeast.

Figure 9: Central American Refugee Routes

More recently a new route has been used, also in the north of Brazil, in the state of Roraima, which borders Venezuela. Mainly Venezuelans and Cubans have arrived by using it. The latter group fly to Caracas and proceed toward the Brazilian border crossing by bus.

In the south of Brazil, a triple border crossing in Foz do Iguaçu that connects Brazil, Argentina, and Paraguay is sometimes used. For those who take a chance at sea, the ports of Santos and Rio de Janeiro are new points of entry.

BRAZILIAN CHURCH'S RESPONSE

The Brazilian church, both Catholic and evangelical, is not passive in relation to refugees' needs. Since the 1930s, through the Scalabrinian Mission in São Paulo, Catholics have pioneered ministries among vulnerable migrants. In addition, CARITAS stands out in its services for refugees in partnership with the UNHCR. The work is very recent among evangelicals, starting around 2010 with the crises in Haiti and Syria. Mission agencies, Christian NGOs, and churches have gradually been getting involved in refugee support efforts in many ways in different cities.

AEBVB, SERVOS, and MAIS have offered part of their facilities to receive refugee families for a period of time. LAR (Cabo Frio/RJ), DIGNITÀ (São Paulo/SP), and CAEBE (Curitiba/PR) opened transitional housing for refugees.

COMPASSIVA (São Paulo/SP) offers advice and guidance in the regularization of degrees and offers Portuguese lessons. Some universities have started enrolling refugees in their programs, such as UNIEVANGÉLICA (Anápolis/GO) and UNICESUMAR (Maringá/PR). ANAJURE, DIGNITÀ, and MAIS have been offering legal assistance in order to enable persecuted Christians to get an entry visa to Brazil. Additionally, TAARE (Uberlândia/MG), MEAB (Foz do Iguaçu/PR), PREPARANDO O CAMINHO (São Paulo/SP), SIM (Londrina/PR), MIAF (São Paulo/SP), JOCUM (Campinas/SP), PROJETO GAIO (Pompeia/SP), and NO MORE (Maringá/PR) have been serving refugees in different ways. In some cities (e.g., São Paulo, Curitiba, Maringá, and Uberlândia), churches are opening their doors to refugees and offering a wide range of services in their own language. Refugees themselves are taking initiative to support others (BAB SHARK), including an incubator to enable them to open their own businesses (BLUE FIELDS).

Some have begun a resettlement program (MAIS and DIGNITÀ), helping and guiding families even before their arrival in Brazil. This program is established in partnership with local churches that offer to "adopt" refugee families for a certain period (one to three years), providing a home, food, Portuguese language lessons, job search assistance, and pastoral care. This model has been successful in integrating refugees into the community. The church functions as an extended family and builds a bridge between refugees and society at large. Dozens of churches of different denominations and cities are part of this program.

Inspired by the example of the Refugee Highway Partnership, some of these organizations have begun to interact, exchange experiences, and encourage each other—taking the first steps toward the creation of a network of refugee ministries in Brazil. This network is called REMIR (*Rede Evangélica de Apoio ao Migrante e Refugiado*, or the Evangelical Network for Supporting Migrants and Refugees) and has more than twenty members, which include churches, mission agencies, and NGOs. The network has convened three major gatherings in Brazil in the last few years to cross-pollinate ideas and to resource and expand their ministries to refugees.

DIFFICULTIES FACING REFUGEES IN BRAZIL

Brazil has yet to develop an intentional and organized program for refugee resettlement, as has been done in the United States, Canada, and Australia. Establishing annual quotas and providing structure and support for those who arrive cause much difficulty for refugees as well as the host society. Brazil's policy of open legislation to receive applicants without any kind of control or planning makes the system itself inefficient and confusing. Depending on the international crisis, the demand is generally more than the service capacity. This was what happened with Haitians and Syrians in 2014 and with Venezuelans in 2017.

Without adequate personnel and resources for serving refugees, in most cases applicants are on their own or at the mercy of other people. There are no organized structures or processes to serve refugees effectively. And NGOs, most of which are religious (Catholic, evangelical, and Islamic), also lack resources and structure.

LACK OF INFORMATION

Refugees who arrive in Brazil know very little about the country or people. The fact that there is no means to inform people about Brazil's refugee system results in much confusion. Refugees get frustrated when they realize that no financial help is available from the government. Most face the challenge of communicating in Portuguese; because of their unfamiliarity, some think they will be able to communicate using English in Brazil. However, this barrier is overcome by Brazilian kindness. Even without understanding the language of refugees, Brazilian agencies are eager to help.

ECONOMY

Since 2015, Brazil has been experiencing an acute political and economic difficulties. As many companies folded up in recent years, the unemployment rate rose to 14 percent, and the cost of living has skyrocketed in big cities. The informal sector ends up being the only alternative for the survival of the refugees and in some cases, vulnerable new refugees end up being exploited and victimized by the slave labor market.

Many refugees find jobs in the civil construction sector, as that offers the most opportunities, but it involves low-paying manual labor. It is difficult for refugees to support a family on a single income. Others, however, find jobs in smaller cities in the interior, where the cost of living is lower. And some acquire jobs in the agricultural sector in rural areas. When the political crisis is over the economy will certainly grow again, which will be a good scenario for those who have already adapted to the culture and mastered the language.

BUREAUCRACY

Many who have applied for refugee status and have a higher level of education have found that their degrees are not recognized by the local government. Thus they can't find a job in their field, or if they do get a job in their field, they receive a much lower salary for the position. This situation has caused some NGOs to demand improvement, and some progress has already been achieved.

XENOPHOBIA AND RACISM

Like many other countries, the Brazilian society is experiencing polarization and the resurgence of fundamentalism, whether political, social, or religious. Xenophobic arguments coming from Europe and the United States are repeated on social media. In the streets, however, this still has little impact, although we have had some sporadic events of aggression and verbal abuse against foreigners. Fortunately, such incidents result in greater levels of solidarity among Christians and society at large. Most of the verbal attacks and opposition weren't directed toward white migrants (Syrians, Iraqis), but toward Haitians and black Africans. This shows a kind of racism that is hardly accepted by most Brazilians. The church can and must be a channel for discussing these hidden societal issues and serve as an agent of healing and reconciliation.

CRIMINALITY AND URBAN VIOLENCE

The big Brazilian cities suffer from an epidemic of violence on account of criminal networks involved in the drugs and weapons trade. If migrants don't get the protection and support of humanitarian organizations, they easily become vulnerable to street gangs. Money can be earned easily through criminality, especially drug trafficking and prostitution. I have personally rescued three young Syrian men who were drawn into male prostitution by local gang leaders and drug lords.

CONCLUSION

I am certain that the hand of God is behind the large-scale forceful displacement of people that we are seeing in our world nowadays. The church, in some countries, is called to receive vulnerable pilgrims. In many others, the church itself is on the road—hungry, helpless, and vulnerable. In both cases, we are called as God's people to discern what the Father is doing, making ourselves available to serve outsiders, as if they were Christ himself (Matt 25:35). For us, the church in the welcoming country, refugees present a concrete opportunity of obedience to the Word: "So show your love for the alien" (Deut 10:19); expfraternity; "Let us do good to everyone, and specially to the family of faith" (Gal 6:10); hospitality, or "friend to the stranger" (Heb 13:2); and the care of orphans, widows, foreigners, and the poor (Zech 7:10).

I am a witness that those who welcome these refugees are equally or even more blessed in this process, in spite of the complex and costly work involved in welcoming them. Our faith is put into practice, our priorities are reordered, our love for the Master and the church is put in perspective, and our vision of the kingdom is magnified. In other words, refugees are blessings in disguise sent by the Father to revitalize our churches. About them, the apostle Peter said: "The Spirit of glory rests upon you" (1 Pet 4:14).

What should we say about the thousands coming to us looking for refuge? What should the church's attitude be toward these foreigners? How should we respond? Isn't it, then, a way to show them Christ's love, right here, in our backyard? Many of them have never had personal contact with a Christian, have never held a Bible. What an opportunity to share the love of Christ!

We serve a God who is the creator of all human beings and the protector of their dignity. I believe that Brazil can be used even more by God as a safe place for those who are in search for a shelter. Since the doors are closed in Western countries, Brazil, with its flexible legislation and thriving church, finds itself in a strategic place to extend hospitality and help for the most vulnerable in our world. More than offering shelter and work, our role is to pastor and disciple the wounded sheep of Jesus, because we are one flock and have only one pastor.

The four youths in the first Syrian family I received in my church have not only become Christians but decided to be missionaries to other refugees. Our Lord is creative, and his plans are much higher than ours. He loves the nations and is intentionally moving to make his love known among all people. God is doing new things even in the midst of wars, natural disasters, persecution, and the forceful scattering of people in our world, just as it was in the first century, as we read in the accounts of the Acts of the Apostles.

chapter nine

Learning from Refugee-led Ministries in Boston

TORLI HARLAN KRUA

"It was God!" or "God brought me here to Boston!" or "It was a miracle!" are claims I have heard repeatedly from refugees and asylum seekers I have interacted with in Boston over the last thirty years. Deeply aware that God was behind their displacement, these refugees are quick to acknowledge the supernatural providences, divine protection, and sustaining power of God that they have experienced along the treacherous trails of seeking shelter. The forceful dislocation, dangerous journeys, and prolonged uncertainties of wandering bring them closer to divine realities and the sovereign acts of God. Many also experienced real encounters with the risen Christ amid these diasporic movements.

These refugees continue to wonder why they, out of the millions of refugees out there, managed to escape war-torn nations and resettle in the peaceful suburbs of Boston. Why were they chosen when so many did not have that chance? Why did they survive when so many perished along the way?

And who is responsible for the influx of refugees? How should Christians and churches engage with the growing number of people forcibly displaced around the world or fleeing war, persecution, or natural disasters?

In 2016, refugees came to Boston from the countries of Iraq, Somalia, Burma, Haiti, the Democratic Republic of Congo, and other places.[1] Since 2009, the number of refugees arriving in Massachusetts each year has

---

[1] Massachusetts Office of Refugees and Immigrants, 2016 Annual Report, 6.

averaged between 1,400 and 1,900. Since 2007, a total of 16,116 refugees have settled in Massachusetts. During this period, Iraqis comprise the largest group of refugees to settle in Massachusetts—more than 4,500. The other major groups during the same time period are Bhutanese (3,000), Somalis (2,100), Burmese (1,800), and Congolese (1,000).

The surprising responses of many refugees and asylum seekers only confirm the prophecy of Jesus in Matthew 24:14—"This gospel of the kingdom will be proclaimed throughout the whole world as a testimony to all nations, and then the end will come" (ESV). This is in sharp contrast, however, to the response of many evangelical Christians in the West—including the United States—who are opposed to refugees entering their nations. Ironically, these Western Christians spend thousands of dollars to send their missionaries to reach "unreached people" all over the world, while remaining unaware that it is God who is actually sending refugees to Western nations. Refugees are a gift of God to Western churches, and that gift needs to be received with gratitude. It make us realize that we all were migrants, like the Israelites in the Promised Land, and exposes us to the fallacy of self-reliance and material abundance. Sadly, a growing number of Western Christians are resisting the call of God to minister to refugees and, in humility, to learn from them or meaningfully relate to them. Instead, many are caught up in political rhetoric on refugee issues, while others want to stay clear of all controversies—leading to hatred of refugees and considered as unwanted intruders.

A SERIES OF MIRACLES

I was one of the most unlikely persons to become a refugee in Boston. No one can deny that my story is filled with miracles and divine provision—from a remote village in Liberia in West Africa, to work for an international firm in Europe, to being uprooted as a refugee, and now serving refugees in Boston. God led me to choose a life of service dedicated to forgotten and desperate refugees. I now strive to reignite hope in the hearts of many suffering people— both in Boston and in Liberia—and to see their lives transformed. My journey over the last thirty years is nothing short of miracle after miracle. And that is why I love to hear the life stories of refugees, because you see the fingerprints of God all over them. So here is my story.

I was born in Liberia, in the village of Tappita, to Rev. Mahn and Esther Krua. I grew up along a dusty road that led to the village of Ziah, where my father established a Christian mission school and Ziah Faith Baptist Church.

Still today, there is no electricity, paved road, or running water; nor are there any telephones or televisions; and no one owns a car. I surrendered my life to Jesus there. Remote places like Ziah perpetuate illiteracy and poverty, but God miraculously sent me away from there to get an education. With the help of a scholarship from the government of Netherlands, I was able go to Freetown in Sierra Leone to attend the Mano River Union Telecommunications Institute.

After graduation I returned to Liberia to work for the Liberian Telecommunications Corporation. But I was arrested and persecuted because of my ethnicity and close ties to the Boston-based Wang Computer Company. This happened when Charles Taylor, a Boston resident, led a deadly rebellion in Liberia. Under threat of death, I was forced to flee to Brussels, Belgium, where I worked for the European subsidiary of Wang Computers. At the height of the Liberian civil war and my professional career, Wang Computers sent me to the US embassy in Monrovia, Liberia, to help restore computer services.

Although I worked at American embassies in West African countries, the barbarism of the war did not soften the hearts of the Americans to grant me a visa. Not only was I denied a visa multiple times, but other eligible Liberians were also denied visas at the American embassy in Monrovia. Ironically, Liberia is the only African country to be colonized by the American Colonization Society with appropriations from the United States Congress. For over a century, Liberia was established as a refuge for the African diaspora and African Americans fleeing the lynchings and other atrocities of American slavery and racism. In fact, ten presidents of Liberia were African American refugees born and educated in the United States.

The majority of Americans, especially those most against refugees and immigrants, are not aware of the way the US is interwoven with the story of refugee-sending nations. This ignorance fuels a false narrative that people arrive on American shores out of the blue and that Americans do not have any responsibility in the refugee crisis of our times. This disconnect must be addressed if refugees and co-laboring Americans are to build ministries that reveal God's hand in our world and genuinely address the contemporary humanitarian crisis of refugees.

Back to my story. War was raging in Liberia and I was denied refuge in Gambia and the United States, leaving me stuck with nowhere else to go. But God had other plans. After my last-ditch effort for a visa at the US embassy in Senegal was denied and the West African Peacekeepers secured Monrovia, I returned to war-ravaged Liberia in 1991. Upon my arrival, I discovered that my office had been broken into and ransacked. The thieves had overturned all the furniture in the office, but in flipping over a filing cabinet they had exposed one of my expired passports—which still had a valid US visa! If I could renew my passport, God had miraculously provided a visa for me to go to the United States on a special assignment. So I flew to Sierra Leone, was able to get my passport renewed at the Liberian embassy, and boarded a British Airways flight to Boston.

MIRACLES IN AMERICA

I soon faced an obstacle encountered by many refugees: loneliness and the difficulty of bringing critically ill family members out of danger to receive safety, care, and treatment. Although a refugee, I had entered the United States using a visitor's visa, and therefore I was unable to secure a job or travel freely in and out of the country. So I began advocacy work, hoping to help unite Liberian families in the US with family members separated by war and stranded in refugee camps.

Opposition to these efforts mounted from evangelical Christians who detested refugees. Additionally, the Cold War era US policy welcomed Eastern European Jews, Christians, and political dissidents but was hostile to African refugees, many of whom were Muslims. Without support, I was discouraged and contemplated leaving America. But it was at this juncture that another miracle happened. Back in Liberia, NPFL (National Patriotic Front of Liberia) rebels, led by Charles Taylor, planned to attack and kill my family members. Tipped off, my family fled before the rebels arrived at their home in the rebel stronghold of Tappita. The rebels came and burned our house to the ground, and my parents hid in the forest for three months. During that time, my mother became ill due to kidney failure and was told at a hospital that she would die within fourteen days.

Without community support, a green card or refugee status, it was impossible for me to see my mother again or help her travel to Boston for medical treatment. But after five denials, the US Immigration Services miraculously granted me a single emergency reentry permit to neighboring Ivory Coast, where my family had sought asylum. In Ivory Coast, my mother became critically ill again and was denied a US visa repeatedly for four months, but I never gave up asking. Without access to proper medical care, she was constantly passing out and kept being revived thanks to twenty-four-hour prayer vigils. Eventually God miraculously intervened and my mother was granted a US visa.

When she arrived in Boston, she was unable to stand or walk as she was admitted to the New England Medical Center. After a month of treatment, Esther Krua walked out of the hospital. It was like a resurrection of the dead. Although my mother was told she would die in fourteen days, she has now lived in Boston for over fourteen years!

SERVING REFUGEES

Caring for my mother meant that I must continue with refugee ministry in America despite many challenges and opposition. Soon after my mother came to the US, my father joined us too and I began various refugee-led ministry efforts in Boston. I established an organization called the Universal Human Rights International (UHRI), a multinational advocacy and human rights organization focused on promoting peace and prosperity in Africa along with refugee and immigrant rights in the United States. We worked with thirty-eight nationalities, representing citizens of twenty-nine African nations, addressing the issue of discrimination against African refugees in the United States. At that time Africa had the world's largest refugee population but the least quota of refugees admitted into the US. Largely due to our efforts, the number of African refugees allowed to enter the US grew from 3,500 in 1993 to 25,000 in 2004. The number of Liberian refugees increased from just 8 in 1990 to 8,000 in 2004.

The Boston metropolitan area includes over 61,600 residents born in Africa,[2] which is more than most US metropolitan areas. As an evangelist concerned with bringing the good news of the gospel of Jesus to people who come to America seeking freedom from oppression and a better life, I have worked with my father to plant numerous African congregations in Boston and other US cities with African immigrant or refugee Christians. As a missionary with Missions Door, these African churches are just one expression of the incredible vitality that refugees bring to Boston.

The Haitian community here, which is one of the largest in the US, has started more than seventy churches. Christian refugees who fled persecution in Indonesia have started more than a dozen churches. Cambodians, who fled conflict and genocide in their home country, formed the second-largest Cambodian American community and have planted a number of churches. Spanish-speaking immigrants and refugees have started about one hundred churches in the city of Boston and hundreds more in eastern Massachusetts.

---

2 US Census, 2010. The current number is undoubtedly much larger.

Brazilian immigrants have started over four hundred churches in our city. The exceptional growth and vitality of Christianity in Greater Boston is called a "quiet revival" and remains hidden to non-refugee and non-immigrant communities, although it is the heart of kingdom growth in our region.

LEARNINGS FROM REFUGEES

The Emmanuel Gospel Center was the first to identify this "quiet revival" happening in our midst, and in 2015 my informal partnership with them led to an invitation to codirect the Greater Boston Refugee Ministry (GBRM). GBRM seeks to build bridges between refugees and churches in mutually transformative relationships that build the capacity of churches to address the local and global refugee crisis together. To date, GBRM has trained about 350 people from seventy-five congregations in the Boston, Lynn, and Lowell areas that minister to refugees. Leaders from about sixty of those churches are involved in an ongoing ministry with over one hundred refugees.

Truly mutually transformative relationships are a foundational element of GBRM—the reality that non-refugees have as much to gain (if not more) from coming alongside refugees than refugees have to gain from the non-refugees who want to help them. At our reflection and evaluation sessions, this idea has been confirmed in real life, as our volunteers share how relating to their newfound refugee friends has blessed and enriched their lives and spiritual growth. In fact, Westerners deprive themselves of a gift from God and the experience of being witnesses to great persecutions and miracles when they do not engage refugees. Christians need to be present and share in the suffering and joy, which results in refugees being born into God's family and lukewarm Christians being jolted awake into God's ongoing mission in the world.

The deep-seated resistance to see refugees as assets in our communities is rooted in history, culture and theology. The current refugee resettlement system and the Western response to the world refugee crisis (secular or Christian) is broken and unsustainable because it is *patronizing*. It does not incorporate input from or leadership of the refugees and is unsustainable since it does not address the root causes of the refugee crisis. Jesus said, "Blessed are the peacemakers, for they will be called children of God" (Matt 5:9). Because love is the hallmark of Christians, we need to boldly step in and create a new refugee system—an extended family that welcomes all refugees and equips former refugees as change agents to go back to the source of the conflict in their war-ravaged homelands to address issues of social and economic injustices and bring the gospel of peace and reconciliation to nations torn apart by hatred, violence, and greed. It is happening in many places already, but without the involvement or knowledge of the broader church.

What will it take for mission agencies and refugee resettlement organizations serving refugees to incorporate refugees in their board leadership or senior management? One core barrier that we see is money; financial realities are often behind discrimination and anti-refugee power dynamics. For example, the missionary funding model makes it difficult for refugees and immigrants—who don't have the financial support networks of white evangelical Christians—to participate functionally in ministry to refugees. Such institutional systems need to be totally overhauled and replaced with more just and inclusive structures.

CONCLUSION

God is bringing refugees to us. Once this fact is understood and appreciated by all Christians, we shall begin to embrace and engage people who are not only loved by God but also sent by God to bless our churches, cities, and nations. Then, together with refugees, we shall embark on a new journey, inspired and motivated by God's miraculous works in the lives of refugees and people all over the world.

SECTION B:

Responses (Advocacy, Counseling, Justice, Peacemaking, and Solidarity)

chapter ten

Standing in Solidarity: Canada's Welcoming Consensus

MARTIN WIGHTMAN

A welcoming attitude is considered part of being Canadian. This is a country where diverse cultures, faiths, and backgrounds are tolerated and even celebrated. However, there is a myth in this image as well as truth.

Canada regularly has welcomed refugees as part of its humanitarian commitments and international obligations. Major influxes of refugees from overseas have included Mennonites, Doukhobors, and Jews from Russia in the late 1800s and early 1900s; European refugees following the Second World War; Hungarians after the revolution of 1956; Uganda's South Asians in the 1970s; the Indochinese "Boat People" in the late 1970s and early 1980s; Kosova refugees in the late 1990s; and Syrian refugees in 2015–16.

Yet the record of welcome is not unblemished. For example, Canada was unwilling to help Europe's Jews prior to World War II. Indeed, for much of the first hundred years after Confederation in 1867, Canada's immigration policy was explicitly discriminatory, based on either race or religion. In recent decades, however, Canada's openness to immigration and willingness to help refugees based on need alone have been comparatively robust.

Canada almost always serves as a final destination for refugees. For reasons of geography, it is not often a first country of refuge or asylum. Though some refugees may be welcomed to Canada on a temporary basis, most are resettled and awarded immediate permanent residency. They are given financial support, through various channels, for one year to cover expenses while they establish themselves. Refugees arriving in Canada are granted temporary health care coverage by the government, and then they proceed to full coverage in their residential province under Canada's universal public health care system. Most have options of attending free language classes and accessing employment assistance. For government-assisted refugees, these services are provided by government-contracted organizations across Canada.

Christians often have been at the forefront of Canada's refugee resettlement efforts. One important and unique tool allowing Canadian Christians and churches to get involved directly in refugee resettlement is the Private Sponsorship of Refugees Program. Under this program, community or religious organizations, or groups of five or more adults, can sponsor a refugee's or refugee family's resettlement to their community. This is a one-year obligation, plus the preparatory time while the government processes the sponsorship application. According to the official website on the topic.

Private sponsors normally support the sponsored refugees by providing the cost of food, rent and household utilities and other day-to-day living expenses; providing clothing, furniture and other household goods; locating interpreters; selecting a family physician and dentist; assisting with applying for provincial health-care coverage; enrolling children in school and adults in language training; introducing newcomers to people with similar personal interests; providing orientation with regard to banking services, transportation, etc.; and helping in the search for employment.[1]

After the year is up or if the family becomes self-supporting, the formal commitment ends. Still, relationships will continue between refugee and sponsors. Many newcomer families will need occasional help navigating paperwork, school, employment, and Canadian culture. Furthermore, informal friendships between sponsors and newcomers continue long after the formal arrangement is complete.

Private sponsorship in its modern form started in the late 1970s. Its explosion may be traced to an impromptu meeting in a Toronto living room organized by a university professor named Howard Adelman. According to the *Toronto Star*, Adelman invited a group of religious and community leaders to his home to discuss helping Indochinese refugees, whose plight was in the news. Those at the meeting intended to draft a letter to the federal immigration minister, demanding government action. However, two civil servants in attendance informed the group of a recently added provision in Canadian immigration law that allowed groups to sponsor refugees privately. The group set a target of sponsoring fifty refugees. But the meeting was chronicled in *The Globe and Mail*; dubbed as "Operation Lifeline," the project grew quickly across the country.[2]

1 "Guide to the Private Sponsorship of Refugees Program," Government of Canada website, www.cic. gc.ca/english/resources/publications/ref-sponsor/section-2.asp (accessed October 31, 2017).
2 Peter Goodspeed, "Can Canada Duplicate Its Boat People Rescue with Syrian Refugees?" *Toronto Star*, September 26, 2014, www.thestar.com/news/atkinsonseries/2014/09/26/can_canada_duplicate_its_ boat_people_rescue_with_syrian_refugees.html (accessed October 27, 2017).

Figure 10: Primary Refugee-producing and Resettlement Countries

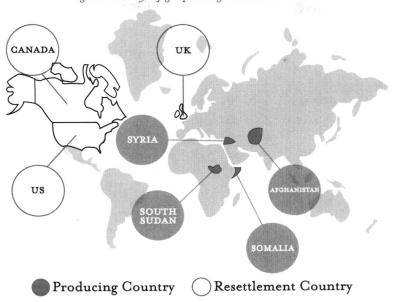

● Producing Country   ○ Resettlement Country

From 1979 to 1980, Canada resettled approximately sixty thousand Indochinese refugees from Vietnam, Cambodia, and Laos. More than half of those were sponsored privately.[3] Christian leaders and churches were key parts of Operation Lifeline and have continued to resettle refugees in Canada, as sponsors and through faith-based organizations that support newcomers. Many churches have programs or partnerships to aid refugees in their first country of asylum.

Although any group of five adults meeting the government's criteria can form a private sponsorship group in Canada, the government also works with larger umbrella organizations, called Sponsorship Agreement Holders. These organizations can work on behalf of multiple subgroups, and they simplify application processes and communication with the government. A significant portion of the Sponsorship Agreement Holders are Christian denominations, individual churches, and Christian organizations.

The number of refugees sponsored privately goes up and down each year, based on both government targets and the interest of sponsoring groups. From 2001 until Canada's larger resettlement of Syrians in 2015–16, the number of privately sponsored refugees arriving each year rarely crested five thousand. These relatively modest numbers often reflected limits on applications or delays

---

3 Michael J. Molloy and James C. Simeon, "The Indochinese Refugee Movement and the Launch of Canada's Private Sponsorship Program," *Refuge: Canada's Journal on Refugees* 32, no. 2 (2016): 3–8, https://refuge.journals.yorku.ca/index.php/refuge/article/view/40412.

in processing rather than a lack of sponsorship interest. While the initial ethos of private sponsorship was to bring "additional" vulnerable people to Canada for resettlement—above and beyond the refugees the government sponsored directly itself—at times the government has counted private sponsorships within its total refugee resettlement targets, or offered blended funding programs that combine private and government sponsorship. In such cases, more private sponsorship has meant lower government expenditures but not necessarily more refugees brought to Canada.[4] Canadian Christian leaders therefore often lobby their government to increase its overall commitment to refugees, while encouraging churches to continue to sponsor privately.

In 2014, for example, the Evangelical Fellowship of Canada (EFC) highlighted its concern for Syrian and other Middle Eastern refugees. The EFC penned a statement on the issue and delivered it in early 2015 to the federal minister of immigration. At the same time, the EFC spurred its member denominations to take action via the private sponsorship program.[5] Paul Carline, director of intercultural ministries with the Convention of Atlantic Baptist Churches, was one of many Christian leaders who responded to the EFC's call to action. His organization was already a Sponsorship Agreement Holder with the government. Yet, as he began to talk to churches, the strong positive response surprised him.

"I sent an email saying 'We'll go for fifty,'" said Carline in an interview, indicating the number of family-unit sponsorships the Atlantic Baptist churches would undertake. "This would've been in January 2015. I had just hit 'send' on that email, and my phone rang, and this gentleman said, 'I'm calling you from Paradise, Nova Scotia. We've never sponsored before, but we feel like we should do this.'"

Carline said that a subsequent meeting in the man's living room was packed, with those in attendance representing many different churches. "Out of that, I think about a dozen families were sponsored, just out of that meeting alone. It was like that in every community that I went to. Community centers would be packed with church people, community people, wanting to know how we could help facilitate them to sponsor refugees."

Similar efforts within churches gained traction throughout 2015. Then the Canadian federal election provided a substantial boost in public interest, as the crisis of Middle Eastern refugees surfaced in the news during the campaign.

---

4 Shauna Labman, "Private Sponsorship: Complementary or Conflicting Interests?" *Refuge: Canada's Journal on Refugees* 32, no. 2 (2016): 67–80, https://refuge.journals.yorku.ca/index.php/refuge/article/view/40266.

5 Anita Levesque, "One Year Later: Evangelical Churches in Canada and Middle Eastern Refugee Sponsorship by the Numbers," The Evangelical Fellowship of Canada website, January 24, 2017, https://www.evangelicalfellowship.ca/Communications/Articles/January-2017/One-Year-Later-Evangelical-Church-in-Canada-and-S (accessed October 30, 2017).

The Liberal Party won the election, in part because of its more open policy proposals on refugee issues. New prime minister Justin Trudeau promised to bring twenty-five thousand Syrian refugees to Canada for resettlement by the end of 2015—just a few months later. At Toronto's airport ahead of the arrival of a flight of Syrian refugees, Trudeau said, "This is a wonderful night where we get to show not just a planeload of new Canadians what Canada is all about, we get to show the world how to open our hearts and welcome in people who are fleeing extraordinarily difficult situations."[6]

Many Christians and churches helped as these planeloads of government-assisted refugees from Syria arrived. "During the Syrian refugee response it was the church that responded first, and in many cases came to us asking how they could help," says Jill Keliher, former managing director of the Saint John YMCA Newcomer Connections Centre, an agency contracted to provide resettlement services to government-assisted refugees in Saint John, New Brunswick.

The timeline was ultimately too aggressive, and the government had to reduce its target for resettlement to 10,000 refugees by the end of 2015, which it still did not succeed in achieving. Nevertheless, the target of 25,000 was reached in early 2016, after a frenetic push by both resettlement agencies and private sponsorship groups. By late 2016, more than 35,000 Syrians had arrived in Canada. According to *The Globe and Mail*, 13,138 of those were privately sponsored and an additional 3,576 were supported by a mix of government and private funding.[7]Furthermore, despite the focus on Syrian refugees, some private sponsorship groups opted to bring refugees from other places based on need, readiness, and the amount of time refugees had been waiting for resettlement.

Most of the recent Syrians resettled in Canada identify as Muslim. But many other refugees have brought Christian faith to Canada, both recently and throughout the country's history. Some are refugees specifically because they have been persecuted for their Christian faith in their homelands. These refugees express their faith in different ways, but all have the right to worship as they choose, and they often join churches in their new locations. In larger cities there may be churches that hold worship services in the refugees' native languages.

---

6   "Full Text of Justin Trudeau's Remarks Ahead of Refugees' Arrival," CBC News, December 11, 2015, http://www.cbc.ca/news/canada/toronto/syrian-refugees-justin-trudeau-remarks-1.3360401 (accessed October 27, 2017).

7   Joe Friesen, "Syrian Exodus to Canada: One Year Later, a Look at Who the Refugees Are and Where They Went," *The Globe and Mail*, December 1, 2016, https://beta.theglobeandmail.com/news/national/syrian-refugees-in-canada-by-the-numbers/article33120934/ (accessed October 31, 2017).

Khuram and Nabeela Shahzad are Christians who fled Pakistan and sought asylum in Sri Lanka before being resettled in Canada. After the local newspaper ran a story profiling their newfound liberty to celebrate Christmas, the Shahzads were greeted by strangers on the street. "It was really exciting because everyone stopped and said Merry Christmas, Happy New Year, and everybody welcomed us very warmly," Khuram Shahzad said in a follow-up interview with the paper.[8]

Not only refugees are helped. Such newcomer Christians also enrich the Canadian church with their diversity and unique witness. "The testimony that a refugee family brings to the larger church family is very powerful," says Jill Keliher. "I think it helps the church here in Canada gain a little bit of perspective on what it means to suffer and what it means to be persecuted and marginalized."

For faith communities that have welcomed a refugee family into their membership, assisted in welcoming government-sponsored refugees, or completed the one-year commitment of private sponsorship, there is still more to do. An emerging challenge for newcomers in Canada—highlighted by the Syrian resettlement push—is family reunification. Former refugees often want to bring their relatives to Canada, both for the sake of togetherness and to rescue them from dangerous conditions. Sponsorship Agreement Holders are allowed to directly choose candidates for sponsorship and can in theory coordinate sponsorships for family members who qualify, but the government has often put stringent limits on how many people can be brought into the country this way.

Tom Denton, a refugee advocate based in Winnipeg, Manitoba, told me in an October 2017 email that the recent wave of refugee resettlement is producing an "echo effect" of demand for family reunification. "The cry I am hearing," he wrote, "is 'Let my people in!'" Paul Carline notes, "They are the most successful of all resettlement initiatives, when a family is coming to join a family that's already here. I don't think there should be a cap on that."

The recent changes may begin to address this; the Canadian government committed in late 2017 to increasing immigration over a multiyear period, part of which includes a significant commitment to family reunification.[9] When there is reluctance from those in government, it usually reflects a degree of resistance from parts of the Canadian public when immigration numbers are increased. Threats to Canadian safety are alleged. Concerns are raised about the values of

8 Kelsey Pye, "Saint John Opens Arms to Newcomers," *The Telegraph-Journal*, January 5, 2015, https://www.telegraphjournal.com/telegraph-journal/story/40731233/saint-john-opens-arms (accessed October 30, 2017).

9 Nicholas Keung, "Canadian Government to Raise Annual Immigration Intake by 13 Percent by 2020," *Toronto Star*, November 1, 2017, https://www.thestar.com/news/immigration/2017/11/01/canadian-government-to-raise-annual-immigrant-intake-by-13-by-2020.html (accessed November 29, 2017).

newcomers (often, though not exclusively, in reference to Muslims). Others argue that the financial cost of resettlement and integration into Canadian society is too high and that the needs of Canada's own marginalized people must be given priority. Many Christians involved in refugee resettlement describe the latter concern as a false dichotomy. Instead, sponsoring refugees can motivate people to be more attentive to the needs of their Canadian neighbors.

Jan O'Hearn has been part of a private refugee sponsorship partnership in Toronto. For her, the experience of sponsorship illuminated new opportunities closer to home. "What my own personal journey has been, as part of this, is by reaching out to refugees—people from other countries, who've experienced such oppression that they are forced to leave their home—it's really brought to light some of our more domestic issues. I am currently interested in how it is we as a society are serving our own oppressed people, specifically marginalized and indigenous people."

Refugee-sponsorship projects often are spearheaded by faith communities or individuals who believe they are called to love their neighbor—both at home and far away. "I think it's just part of the responsibility that we have to people who are poor or find themselves war-torn, the foreigner, the orphan—those are the people God asks us to help," says Jennifer Epp. With her husband, Mark, Jennifer has been part of a church group near Vancouver that sponsored a Syrian refugee family in cooperation with the Mennonite Central Committee.

Paul Carline encourages refugee-sponsoring churches not to stop. "Now our challenge to those churches is: 'Don't let this be your grand gesture. Who are the next people that God wants you to open your eyes and see?'"

Although Canada sometimes has ignored needy people, the country nevertheless has shown a willingness to help refugees. Canadian Christians and churches have been on the front lines in the challenging and rewarding task of welcoming the stranger. In the process, many communities have been blessed, rejuvenated, and transformed. And many refugees have found a new home.

chapter eleven

Welcoming Refugees for the Glory of God in Germany

DR. PETER VIMALASEKARAN

As a result of wars, terrorism, and political instabilities in Iraq, Syria, and Afghanistan, a record number of people have been forced to flee their homelands and seek shelter in Europe, often entering through Greece. In 2016, this created a meltdown of attitudes toward refugees in many European countries. Germany took in nearly one million refugees during this period and showed the world that it is possible to care for refugees at this critical juncture. According to Germany's Federal Statistical Office, "On 31 December 2016, 1.6 million people seeking protection were registered in Germany. They accounted for 16 percent of the country's foreign population. Based on the Central Register of Foreigners, the number of people seeking protection increased by 851,000 (+113 percent) since the end of 2014."[1]

The German government was very efficient in organizing unexpected arrivals of thousands of refugees and providing them with shelter, food, and even generous pocket money. The Syrian refugees who came to Germany were granted asylum quicker than refugees from other countries. Many Germans welcomed refugees and supported Angela Merkel's open door policies. Some of the restrictive laws affecting refugees were changed, and academic institutions invited refugees to study. Several businesses, including Bosch and Siemen, offered training to refugees. However, the arrival of refugees also increased intolerance, nationalism, and populism in formerly open European nations.[2]

---

1 Federal Statistical Office, "Migration and Integration," https://www.destatis.de/EN/FactsFigures/ SocietyState/Population/MigrationIntegration/MigrationIntegration.html (accessed January 13, 2018).

2 Erik Berglof, "The Evolution of the Refugee Crisis," *Handelsblatt*, https://global.handelsblatt.com/ opinion/the-evolution-of-the-refugee-crisis-869918 (accessed January 9, 2018).

A few negative incidents have turned the good will of the people against the ruling political party, and in 2017 an anti-immigrant party won several seats in the German parliament for the first time.

GOD CARES FOR REFUGEES

In the Scriptures, God exhorted his people Israel to care for and support the strangers who lived in their midst:

> "You shall not wrong a sojourner or oppress him, for you were sojourners in the land of Egypt" (Ex 22:21 ESV).
>
> "You shall not strip your vineyard bare, neither shall you gather the fallen grapes of your vineyard. You shall leave them for the poor and for the sojourner: I am the Lord your God" (Lev 19:10 ESV).
>
> "When a stranger sojourns with you in your land, you shall not do him wrong. You shall treat the stranger who sojourns with you as the native among you, and you shall love him as yourself, for you were strangers in the land of Egypt: I am the Lord your God" (Lev 19:33–34 ESV).

God openly declare his love for strangers: "He executes justice for the fatherless and the widow, and loves the sojourner, giving him food and clothing" (Deut 10:18 ESV). God commanded his people to care for the strangers living among them.

In the New Testament, we read that Jesus was a refugee who had to escape to Egypt because of Herod's murderous plans (Matt 2:1–15). No wonder Jesus identified with the uprooted and fleeing people of the world. He spoke about his disciples giving food to the hungry and drink to the thirsty, welcoming strangers, clothing the naked, and visiting the sick and those in prison. And then he stated, "As you did it to one of the least of these my brothers, you did it to me" (Matt 25:36–40 ESV).

Throughout the Bible we see many different forms of displacement of people and how they served distinctive kingdom purposes. The biblical words for "strangers" can be translated "temporary residents"—those who are outside their home—or "migrants"—those who have fled to safety. According to Burt Singleton, "No distinction is made in scripture as to whether the alien/ stranger has arrived simply as one on a journey or rather has fled war, political persecution, ethnic prejudice or starvation."[3]

---

3 Burt Singleton, "Finding and Ministering to Refugees," in *The Refugees Among Us: The Unreached Peoples '83*, ed. Edward R. Dayton and Samuel Wilson (Monrovia, CA: MARC, 1983), 61–76.

THE CHURCH'S RESPONSE TO REFUGEES

The church of Christ cannot idly stand by and think that the refugee issue will be handled by government agencies and private charities. Believers have a great opportunity to show the love of Christ by serving refugees. It is important that we don't see refugees as mere gospel targets, but rather truly care for their physical and spiritual needs holistically. Ronald Mummert writing in 1992, prophetically and correctly exhorted, "The world refugee problem is a terrible one which may even worsen as social, political, economic, and environmental upheavals continue. Thus, the church needs to consider the refugee ministry a viable addition to congregational mission programs."[4] In other words, having a refugee ministry is essential for every congregation as we reach out to strangers in our midst.

We must see refugee ministries as a God-given opportunity to fulfill the Great Commission mandate to share the gospel with people unlike ourselves. Stephanos Tedla, writing in 1985, prophetically contended, "Refugees, perhaps, more than any other group of people today, embody human suffering and vulnerability. Uprooted and homeless, they bear in their persons the marks of the suffering Christ, wounded, despised without a place to rest."[5]

While Scripture does not equate poverty with holiness or a close walk with God (see Job 1:3; 42:12–16), Christians frequently experience hardships and ostracization in a fallen world, as their Lord did. And God asks us to have genuine concern for and serve all people who have come under hard times.

MY REFUGEE JOURNEY

I am no stranger to the stories of many refugees with whom I work. I was born into a multi-religious family in the small town of Mannar in Sri Lanka. Like other children in my community, my childhood was spent going to school and playing cricket. All that changed when I became a teenager, however, as the civil strife between the majority people and the minority Tamils started to ravage our land. As the conflict intensified, many from my Tamil community feared for their lives, as they were suspected of aiding the Tamil rebel groups and were arrested, detained, or simply disappeared. Young people were particularly affected by this brewing civil war, and I had to escape to the neighboring country of India with my parents and siblings.

---

4 J. Ronald Mummert, with Jeff Bach, *Refugee Ministry in the Local Congregation* (Scottdale, PA: Herald Press, 1992), 46.

5 Stephanos Tedla, "The Refugee Problem in Africa," *African Ecclesial Review* 27 (1985): 115–19.

Though I had a very difficult time during the civil war, I would concur with the psalmist, "It is good for me that I was afflicted, that I might learn your statutes" (Ps 119:71 ESV). Through the times of uncertainty and pain that I experienced, the love of Christ changed me forever to serve him.

After four years of living as refugees, my family and I returned to our homeland. Through various circumstances, God led me to study theology in England, Northern Ireland, and the United States and then called me to minister to refugees. Along with my wife and our four children, since 1998 I have been in Germany serving refugees and migrants in various capacities and in different cities.

Figure 11: Refugee Sea Routes to Europe (2015)

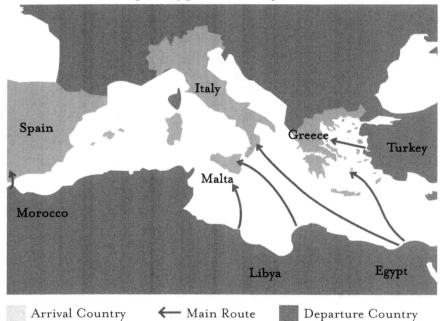

EVANGELICAL REFUGEE CENTER IN KARLSRUHE (GERMANY)

In 2011, European Christian Mission Refugee Ministry moved us from Freiburg to Karlsruhe to work among refugees and support local churches engaging in refugee ministries. Karlsruhe is home to the first registration center for the province of Baden Wuerttemberg, which takes in 12.5 percent of refugees who come to Germany. After processing the necessary details for their asylum applications, refugees are moved to various refugee camps in the province. When we arrived in Karlsruhe, no evangelical churches were engaged in ministry to refugees at the registration center, although one individual had faithfully visited refugees for several years.

We were able to raise awareness and help local churches engage in refugee ministry. Several evangelical churches gladly opened their doors to refugees and helped them with their many practical needs. This led to various meetings, language teaching, informal café gatherings, etc. However, we needed a central place to coordinate activities on a daily basis and to help refugees integrate into German culture and faith communities. As Christians, we wanted to show the love of God in action to refugees—without discrimination based on refugees' cultural backgrounds, race, or religious convictions, but also not compromising our Christian witness.

By the providence of God, some evangelical churches, a state church, and our local refugee ministries joined together to establish the Evangelical Refugee Center in Karlsruhe in November 2016. A formal agreement was signed by all the leaders at an opening ceremony. This was one of the first joint projects between the state church and the evangelical churches in the province.

The idea of a refugee center is to provide a stable environment both for refugees who have just arrived in Germany and for those who have been living in the area for several years. It brings together German Christians from various churches and neighborhoods to enhance interaction with refugees. As resettlement agencies have taken care of housing, food, and language/ skill training, what refugees really need is long-term relational investment and the development of friendships between the host society and themselves. The refugee center provides a platform for caring Christians to interact with refugees, bear witness to Jesus Christ, and fulfill his command to love and care for the needy and vulnerable in our society. Our aim is to provide a space for refugees and local people to meet, get to know one another, and appreciate each other without being threatened by the newcomers.

The mission of the Evangelical Refugee Center is to:

1. Provide regular help and support to the refugee volunteer workers. The center conducts training for refugee volunteer workers once a month.

2. Conduct orientation classes to help refugees adapt to life in their new country. These classes help refugees understand the German way of life, culture, and laws and acquire other important information.

3. Assist refugees in obtaining basic German language competence and support them in finding jobs.

4. Support refugee women and children though group meetings and other activities specifically prepared for them.

5. Advocate for refugees by organizing special events on refugee issues and needs. This includes Refugee Sunday, special prayer meetings, and awareness events.

6. Take local believers to camps to get to know refugees. The welcome team regularly organizes visits to refugee camps in Germany by obtaining required permissions and clearances.

7. Organize Christian events for refugees, such as Christmas and Easter programs.

8. Help local churches get involved in refugee ministry. Many churches want to serve refugees but don't know how to go about it. Our center is able to assist churches in increasing their level of involvement with refugees.

9. Offer trauma counselling to refugees. Most refugees have shown extreme levels of psychological problems; we are in the early stage of finding ways to help refugee families.

10. Establish community cafés where refugees and church members come together to cook different cuisines, play their national games, and harness support for refugees. This also enables German believers to know their new neighbors by sharing their lives with refugees.

DIASPORA MISSION TO AND THROUGH REFUGEES

The Lausanne Movement's Cape Town congress in 2010 called for "Mission from everywhere to everywhere," and this aptly fits refugee ministry in Germany. It is no longer a question of why refugees are in our neighborhoods, as many have arrived from many countries that are closed to the gospel and where missionaries are not allowed. On account of war and political turmoil, they escape from their homelands to come into European countries where they can freely hear the good news of the Lord Jesus Christ. This is particularly true in the case of many Iranians, Afghans, Syrians, and Kurds, as well as other unreached people groups.

In other words, refugee movements are providential acts of God for sharing his love with people. Not only that, many refugees have become witnesses of the Lord Jesus Christ to their own people as well to their host nations. For example, many Sri Lankan Tamils who fled thirty years of civil war to many European nations, North America, and other parts of the world have heard the gospel and become followers of Jesus Christ. Many Sri Lankan churches in Germany (and in other European countries, Canada, and the US) have reached out to their own people and to their host nations. During the years of civil war in Sri Lanka, the western Tamil Christian diaspora played a significant part in supporting Christians and their churches in the northern part of Sri Lanka. At the same time, many second generation Sri Lankan Tamils are now part of German churches and helping them become mission-minded. There are many refugee churches among Iranians, Nepalis, Pakistanis, Somalis, Eritreans, Syrians, Kurds, and others in Germany.

This is the unprecedented plan of God in reaching lost people wherever they go and wherever they live. The refugee arrivals in Europe have stirred many churches into mission work, and refugees have created new vitality in many European churches. Many monoethnic churches in Germany have become multiethnic churches and have embraced God's new plan for their faith community. The refugees have become evangelists to reach their own people and other refugees, which has brought about a much-needed spirit of renewal to dormant churches in Europe. Though some churches have been opposed to refugee arrivals and have closed their doors to refugees, the overall impact of refugees has been positive in many cities of Germany.

CONCLUSION

The recent refugee crisis is unlike anything we have ever seen in the world. People are on the move, and God is on the move with them. God's sovereign plans are not thwarted by human actions; rather, God continues to build the church through exceptional ways. "I know that you can do all things, and that no purpose of yours can be thwarted." (Job 42:2 ESV).

Who would have thought that God could redeem what we call the greatest humanitarian crisis for his glory by drawing thousands to himself? God cares for refugees and is at work among refugees. God's family must do the same by serving the refugees arriving in our cities. This is an opportunity presented to us to show the world that our God cares for refugees and has a special plan for their future. Mission agencies and local churches should work together in caring for refugees in every possible way. By doing so, we fulfill God's command to reach the nations at our doorstep and help congregations catch a vision for global missions.

chapter twelve

Ministry to Refugees Arriving in Europe

Daniel Zeidan

The refugee crisis in Europe has captured the world's attention in recent years. In late 2015, after several months of wide-ranging relief work for thousands of refugees who made the perilous sea journey from Turkey to the Greek islands on a daily basis, Samaritan's Purse initiated an outreach program for refugees called "The Meeting Place" (TMP). The aim of the initiative was to ensure that the thousands of refugees arriving in Europe received much-needed humanitarian assistance and a clear presentation of the gospel.

The vision of TMP sprang out of a need to create a transitional safe place for refugees journeying through Europe where they would feel welcomed, respected, and listened to and where they could hear the good news. It was felt that Europe's refugee crisis had created a historically unprecedented window of opportunity for sharing the saving message of the gospel with some of the least-reached people on earth—a segment of the world's population that would otherwise be in "closed" or "restricted access" countries hostile to the gospel and Christian mission. The idea was to continue meeting the physical needs of refugees in camps run by the Greek authorities, while introducing a more intentional evangelistic component to the emergency response.

The first TMP center was set up in a large tent at the Galatsi refugee camp just outside of Athens, Greece. It provided free snacks, Wi-Fi, cellular charging stations, and a warm and welcoming space for refugees to sit and chat with experienced staff who spoke Dari and Arabic. A second TMP center was soon established in the refugee transit camp in Slavonski Brod in Croatia. Through these initial efforts in late 2015, some 7,055 refugees were served by TMPs, and

470 were personally presented with the gospel, of which 96 surrendered their lives to Jesus Christ.

The evangelistic activities were discreetly carried out in the Galatsi and Slavonski Brod camps with the permission of the authorities. However, in early 2016, following the closure of the Galatsi camp in Athens and the introduction of tighter regulations over "proselytizing activities," the decision was made to find more permanent locations for TMP operations outside the camps. TMP searched for suitable sites for setting up coffee shops near refugee hubs in the city center. The rented coffee shops allow greater freedom to manage activities and share the gospel openly, while continuing to serve as safe spaces for refugees.

A SIMPLE VISION

The vision that sprang up in the fall of 2015 and developed in early 2016 was simple: create a place of refuge along the refugee travel routes in Europe where refugees could stop in, get some rest, and be embraced by caring staff who understood their culture and language. As staff asked guests to share their story and inquired where they were from, where they were heading to, and what their hopes were for the future, many were willing to talk openly about the treacherous journey they had been through, the conflict and violence they experienced back home, and the new life and security they were hoping to find in Europe. When appropriate, TMP staff asked if they could pray with guests regarding their lives and future. If they showed more interest, they were introduced to Jesus Christ—*Isa al-Masih*,[1] as he is known in Arabic and Farsi.

Nowadays evangelism has become an embarrassing topic for many mainline Christian denominations, not to mention most secular and political entities who frown upon the practice as being intolerant, manipulative, or even unethical. It is considered politically incorrect to talk about evangelism, especially to a Muslim audience. While openly and unashamedly evangelistic in nature, TMP does not espouse aggressive or manipulative methods. Rather, the gospel is shared "with integrity" and "within the context of relationship and with no conditionality."[2] TMP staff self-identify as Christians and are trained never to take advantage of the desperate circumstances of refugees or "capitalize" on their tragedy. They are mandated to treat refugees as human beings, affirming their identity as persons known and loved by God and created in his image.

---

1 Christian Arabs prefer to use the name *Yasu* for Jesus, and this is closer to the original Hebrew *Yeshua*. Some missiologists contend that using the Muslim designation Isa is erroneous, as it refers to the Qur'anic Jesus who is denied of his deity, sacrificial death on the cross, and resurrection. Nevertheless, others point out the positive contextual advantages of using the familiar Isa for Muslim evangelism, at least during the introductory phases.

2 Arthur Brown, "The Refugee and the Body of Christ: The Impact of the Middle East Crisis on Our Understanding of Church," *Lausanne Global Analysis* 5, no. 5 (September 2016): 5.

All TMP services are offered freely and unconditionally to all guests, and it was only through the nurturing of relationships that those interested in the Christian faith were invited to hear more. Some refugees stopped in for a cup of tea and never returned. Others showed signs of physical and emotional exhaustion, either from the arduous journey or from the sordid camp conditions, and dozed off for hours in a warm place where they would not be asked to leave. Still others came to use the bathroom or play a game of chess or table football with their friends before moving on. But many stayed for half a day or longer, and returned the next day to speak to our staff about *Isa*. TMPs offered refugees a semblance of some normalcy and peace, an escape from boredom and the overcrowded camps. Refugees could forget for a few hours the stigma, trauma, and uncertainty of displacement and interact with people who cared and would listen to them.

Figure 12: Top Five Nationalities Arriving by Sea to Europe (2015)

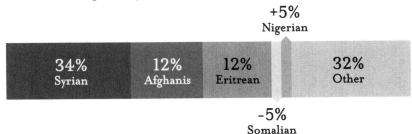

A key to the success of this ministry and its evangelistic impact was the team of experienced evangelists recruited to staff the TMP centers. Staff members were hired from around the globe, from Bolivia to North America, Egypt to South Africa, and India to Australia. They not only had a burning passion to reach Muslims with the gospel, but most had considerable experience working in restricted-access countries and were fluent in Dari, Farsi, or Arabic. They saw the proclamation of the gospel in word, as well as its demonstration through good deeds based upon the biblical mandate to show love to the alien. Christian outreach is incomplete without a verbal presentation of the good news, and together with compassionate care, the gospel becomes very attractive to refugees.

TMP INITIATIVE EXPANDS

After the initial success of TMP centers in Greece, the initiative was expanded to refugee-destination countries in Europe in collaboration with local church partners in places like Austria, Croatia, Germany, and Denmark. The TMP center in Croatia was closed in early 2016 when the migration route was changed. While a major reason for collaborating with local churches stemmed from the sheer logistical and resource constraints of operating multiple TMP centers across several countries in Europe, the shift in strategy proved to be a blessing for both Samaritan's Purse and the church partners. From a practical perspective, it reduced costs and logistical complications considerably. From a strategic and local church perspective, the shift helped motivate, equip, and mobilize church partners to meet the monumental challenge of reaching out to thousands of Muslim refugees settling in their cities and to consider the crisis as a divinely orchestrated mission opportunity. This was fulfilling a key element in our organizational mission to "serve the church worldwide for the promotion of the Gospel of the Lord Jesus Christ."

TMP activities are run or staffed by Farsi-speaking and Arabic-speaking congregations who understand refugee culture and backgrounds. They function under the auspices of larger local or international churches in the host city and act as a welcoming family and community to the newcomers—providing material and nonmaterial (social, emotional, and spiritual) support—who are often viewed as strangers or even as a threat by the European societies. In Cologne, Germany, the Farsi-speaking congregation coordinates special dinners, cultural orientation, sports, and other programs for refugees. In Aalborg, Denmark, the Arabic-speaking congregation organizes summer camps in rural North Jutland for dozens of refugees, inviting them to get out of the tedium of refugee camps. In Vienna, the TMP provides German and English language classes as well as orientation to Austrian culture. These churches, with their intimately knit networks and shared values, form a remarkable source of social capital for refugees, greatly assisting in their integration into the host society.

The typical activities TMPs engage in to serve refugees, apart from the daily provision of free refreshments and Wi-Fi, include language lessons, asylum information, legal aid, cultural orientation, special Christmas and Easter programs, mothers and toddlers programs, sports (football, volleyball, chess tournaments, and gym passes), second-hand clothes, diapers and toys, and providing connections to local churches. Our staff regularly speak to refugees who have been disillusioned not only by their despotic leaders but also by the excesses of sharia law and the intolerance embedded in their religion and sacred texts. Away from the firm grip of religious leaders and communities back home, many associate the suffering and hardships they experienced in their homelands with the culture of violence and hate that the Muslim world is engulfed in. They despise the way their leaders and mullahs have taken entire neighborhoods and communities hostage to sectarian conflict or jihad.

In fact, many refugees who have come to Europe are keen to leave behind their old way of life. They are open to the gospel and are attracted by the love they see expressed by Christians they come across in Europe. Many have expressed genuine interest in the Christian faith and, above everything else, show deep curiosity and admiration for the person and power of Jesus Christ and his message of love.

Unfortunately, the openness they experience in Europe and the autonomy from the restraints of their communities and strict religious systems can be all too intoxicating for some. There is a vast cultural gulf between secular, liberal Europe (which, incidentally, many refugees perceive as "Christian" Europe) and the traditional Muslim societies from which most recent refugees in places like Germany and Sweden come from. The implications are that the sudden exposure to the individualistic culture of Northern Europe and its liberal moral influences also carry with them certain risks—especially for young unmarried men.[3]

At any rate, the destruction and grief they experienced back home, coupled with their current condition of displacement, bring many refugees to question underlying assumptions they have held about life's purpose and about God and lead them to ask profound questions. Some take advantage of the willingness of churches to embrace them, and there are reports of refugees being all too eager to get baptized in order to avoid deportation, claiming their lives would be in danger if they returned to their countries as Christian converts. Hence many churches, including most TMP partners, hold a rigorous six-month Christian orientation course for new believers, which refugees are obliged to attend before being baptized. But overall, even those who enter a church or a TMP center with the wrong motives are impacted by the gospel and the supportive fellowship they experience.

Abbas, a refugee in his mid-forties and a former accountant in the Iranian Ministry of Agriculture, was asked what attracted him to the Christian faith. Abbas explained that for forty-four years Islam had been injected into him every day. He felt the burden of its many regulations and demands heavy on his shoulders. After hearing the gospel, Abbas knew he wanted and needed to take a step of faith and trust Jesus Christ as his Lord and Savior. He said the unconditional love and forgiveness offered by Christ was like nothing he had experienced before. However, he admitted that his upbringing had instilled in him great fear of the consequences of displeasing or abandoning Allah. "If I claim that Jesus is God, Allah will punish me," he confided quietly.

---

3 This includes sexual liberties and the availability of alcohol and illegal substances. As a disproportionate number of recent refugees coming to Europe are unmarried young men, there are many incidents of sexual harassment of local women and other antisocial behaviors perpetrated by young asylum seekers, which leads to anti-refugee backlash. See "Migrant Men and European Women," *The Economist*, January 16, 2016, http://www.economist.com/news/leaders/21688397-absorb-newcomers-peacefully-europe-must-insist-they-respect-values-such-tolerance-and (accessed November 1, 2017).

But Abbas did eventually meet Jesus through TMP and associated with the Farsi-speaking congregation in that city, and he wept as he surrendered his life to him completely.

Like many other migrants who have put their faith in Christ, Abbas knows he has embarked on a journey of transformation. The heavy twin burdens of legalism and fear, which had marked his old life, have been replaced by the easy yoke and light burden of Christ.

Overall, between November 2015 and November 2016 more than 50,000 Muslim refugees were served by the TMP initiative across Europe, and 10,259 of them were directly presented with the gospel.[4] Some 431 accepted Jesus Christ as their Lord and Savior. The following table demonstrates TMP results in Europe during that first year of operation.

Figure 13: The Meeting Place Results by Country (November 2015–November 2016)

Indicator	Greece	Croatia	Austria	Germany	Denmark	Total
Migrants served	39,063	3,047	2,650	2,740	7,201	54,701
Migrants presented with the gospel	3,450	245	684	1,336	4,544	10,259
Migrants prayed for	1,248	199	244	625	2,455	4,771
Migrants who received a Bible	536	0	23	293	582	1,434
Migrants who received Christian literature	1,796	8	0	604	2,852	5,260
Confessions of faith	41	100	27	123	140	431

A SNAPSHOT OF TMP COLOGNE

Germany has become a magnet for refugees, demonstrated by the fact that as many as 1.1 million have sought shelter there.[5] Samaritan's Purse chose Cologne for its refugee outreach mainly due to the city's status as a major urban refuge hub. Cologne was in the news in early 2016 after the apparently organized sexual assaults by gangs of refugee men on local women during the city's New Year's Eve celebrations. It was later reported that at least ten of the suspects were asylum

---

4 The second indicator ("Migrants presented with the gospel") counts those migrants who received a clear verbal presentation of the gospel—i.e., that God loves them, Christ died for them on the Cross, and that they can find restoration and eternal life through the atoning work of Christ.

5 Bruce Katz, Luise Noring and Nantke Garrelts, "Cities and Refugees: The German Experience," The Brookings Institution, https://www.brookings.edu/research/cities-and-refugees-the-german-experience/ (accessed June 20, 2017).

seekers, nine of whom arrived in Germany in the preceding four months at the height of Europe's refugee crisis.[6] Hence anti-immigrant tensions had been simmering in Cologne for some time when TMP began its operations there in March of 2016.

TMP Cologne was established in collaboration with *Evangelische Freikirche Köln*, a church in the outskirts of the city. The church has a mission vision and a growing Farsi-speaking congregation that meets on Sunday afternoons. When presented with the proposal of establishing an outreach to the city's refugees through TMP, the church's leadership jumped at the opportunity, as it fit with their overall vision and existing ministries. Led by Pastor André Töws and Iranian-born Pastor Shahram Adimi, the TMP center was opened and activities soon started to attract particularly Iranian, Afghani, and Yezidi migrants. In the summer of 2016, eighty-eight new refugee believers were baptized, and thirty-two were baptized in early 2017. The congregation has now developed a full-scale baptism preparation class for new converts and a comprehensive discipleship program. Through these outreach activities to refugees, the congregation grew from around eighty members in 2014 to more than four hundred at the end of 2016.

GOD IS AT WORK IN EUROPE

The apparent success of the TMP initiative prompted Samaritan's Purse to expand the program to two additional European cities in 2017: Malmo, Sweden, and Oslo, Norway. As of July 2017, the six TMPs have seen a cumulative total of 21,451 migrants presented with the gospel and 658 surrender their lives to Christ. Although the initiative began as relief in refugee camps, God continues to use this program to bring hundreds of Muslim refugees to a living faith in Jesus Christ.

Moreover, there is growing evidence of thousands of Muslim refugee converts in Europe awakening the stagnant European church to God's power and triggering a spiritual renewal.[7] Many partner churches are experiencing numerical growth through new refugees, but also by a fresh vitality that is being breathed into them as they discover a renewed vision and calling. In this context refugee ministries are playing a catalytic role in the awakening that is washing over the church in Europe, as churches reach out to refugee strangers in their midst.

---

6 "Cologne Attackers Were of Migrant Origin," *BBC News Services*, January 11, 2016, http://www.bbc.com/news/world-europe-35280386 (accessed November 1, 2017).

7 Sam George, "Is God Reviving Europe through Refugees? Turning the Greatest Humanitarian Crisis of Our Times into One of the Greatest Mission Opportunities," *Lausanne Global Analysis* 6, no. 3 (May 2017).

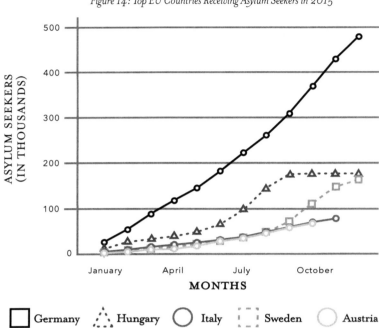

Figure 14: Top EU Countries Receiving Asylum Seekers in 2015

☐ Germany ⋰ Hungary ◯ Italy ⸠ ⸡ Sweden ◯ Austria

Three important lessons emerge from the TMP experience with Europe's refugees. First is the importance of intentionally working with and through local churches to minister to refugees. The partnership with local churches has several practical and logistical advantages. It also harnesses the local church's evangelistic capabilities and resources for a common purpose and calling. And it ensures the sustainability and long-term impact of the ministry to refugees.

Second, in addition to addressing the spiritual needs of refugees, churches facilitate integration into host societies. They are sources of social capital for refugees with its linguistic and cultural affinities with refugees and connection to a native church, a denomination, and other organizations in the host country. The church members and the refugees become part of a larger intimate network of relationships, offering mutual support and cooperation based on shared values and trust.

The third lesson is the importance of not shying away from evangelism, from proclaiming Christ to Muslim refugees. While not taking advantage of refugees' distressed conditions, refugee ministries must present the hope of the gospel and its relevance to people who have experienced extreme trauma, loss, and displacement.

CONCLUSION

On a midsummer night in Athens, Hassan, an Afghan refugee residing in one of the refugee camps, woke up to a cross shining through his tent. Amazed by what he saw and wondering if it was a sign from heaven, Hassan came to TMP, where he was able to ask one of the Dari-speaking staff members about the meaning of the cross he saw. The evangelist explained to Hassan what Jesus did for humanity on the Cross and how Christ's death on the Cross expressed the great love he had not just for the world but for Hassan himself.

Like Hassan until this occasion, more than two million Muslim refugees in Europe have never heard the good news of the gospel. Others have a distorted view of Jesus based on Qur'anic passages that cite Isa as a mere prophet and deny his sacrificial death on the Cross, his resurrection, and his divinity. The calling of every Christian is to reach out to the alien and show love in the name of Christ. But beyond the material help, the largely stagnant church in Europe has an opportunity at this juncture in history to be at the forefront of spiritual renewal, generated by the thousands of Muslims who are turning to Jesus Christ and the fresh fervor and life the new believers are bringing with them.

chapter thirteen

Refugee Children's Ministry in South Sudan

Julia Kapuki Jada

South Sudan became the youngest country in the world when it gained independence from (North) Sudan in 2011, following more than twenty years of guerrilla warfare that claimed the lives of at least 1.5 million people and displaced more than 4 million people. Made up of more than sixty ethnic groups—with their distinct ethnicities, languages, and cultures—South Sudan is one of the most diverse countries in Africa. These groups also differ in matters of religion, social class, sources of livelihood, and rural or urban way of life. The majority of the estimated population of 12 million people are Christians of Catholic background, a small percentage are Muslims, and others hold traditional animist beliefs. Eighty-three percent of the population live in rural areas. The war history played a big role in keeping the people in the rural areas, without any significant development compared to northern Sudan. The prolonged wars have taken a toll on this young nation, as over 4 million citizens have fled their homes to seek help and shelter in other parts of the country and all six neighboring nations.

A year after independence, a major conflict broke out between government and opposition forces, which led to the dire humanitarian emergency of the displacement of millions of South Sudanese and plunged the country back into a major crisis. Economic strife, insecurity, and the lack of food, health care, and other basic needs forced hundreds of thousands of people to flee to Ethiopia, Kenya, Uganda, Congo, and Sudan. Spiraling violence, deteriorating economic conditions, a severe food shortage, and ongoing drought have forced an additional two million people to be internally displaced. The overall situation in

South Sudan at the beginning of 2018 had escalated to a full-blown humanitarian catastrophe.

According to recent UNHCR reports, the total number of South Sudanese refugees outside of their country has surpassed two million. This has become the largest refugee crisis in Africa and the third largest in the world, after Syria and Afghanistan. A large number of South Sudanese refugees are drawn by the generous provisions of land to neighboring Uganda, which now hosts more than one million refugees, putting an enormous strain on that nation's resources and infrastructure. About 65 percent of the refugees are under the age of eighteen, and about 82 percent are women and children. Those who survive are faced with sexual assault, and in many cases children are traveling alone. Some project that by the end of 2018 there will be more than three million South Sudanese refugees, of which nearly two million will be in Uganda alone.

OVERWHELMING NEEDS

As the new nation of South Sudan marked its historic independence on July 9, 2011, its troubles were far from over. That colorful moment was mixed with tears of joy and memories of sadness, recalling the millions who had lost their lives. The celebration also gave life to the dreams of those who had escaped death by running away to neighboring countries or to Europe, Australia, Canada, or the United States—dreams of coming home to a better future after decades of living elsewhere. But these dreams of regaining what they had lost during the war years turned into a nightmare when war erupted again in December 2013 and ethnic conflict and political misunderstanding quickly spread across the nation, leading to the deaths of thousands of men, women, and children.

The needs of the refugees living in camps are greater than the available help or capacity. In light of the major health risks and pervasive poverty, the refugees are utterly dependent on humanitarian aid. They need spiritual and emotional support, as well as financial support. Our people are in desperate conditions and need all kinds of help for sheer survival; emotionally they are broken, full of pain, and hopeless. They cannot trust their own government officials or soldiers—who, instead of protecting people, are exploiting them across ethnic lines. Both the rebel forces and the government soldiers are merciless and eager to harm and even kill people. They not only create fear and force people to flee their homes and villages, but also forcefully steal food, cattle, or any other assets people may have.

Figure 15: Mediterranean Sea Refugee Routes

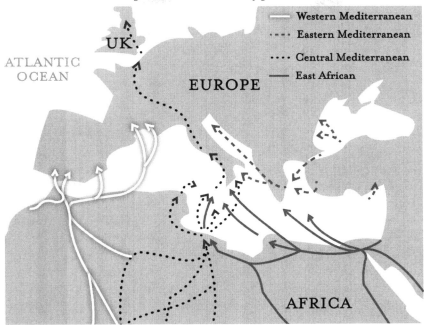

Many family members are separated from each other, including children and their parents. Many young ones have no idea where their parents are or where to go next. The warring factions are recruiting children to be soldiers, and children are abducted for trafficking as the refugee situation becomes even more severe.

For example, I met a young boy in a southern border town who was about six or seven years old and all alone. Some people left him at the border crossing that separates South Sudan and Uganda. The boy was hoping to get across the border. Perhaps he was expecting his parents to meet him on the other side of the border, although he didn't know their whereabouts. He had no idea of the conflicts raging in the country or what it entails to escape to another country as a refugee. So many like him are exploited by traffickers and warring factions.

A young woman recounted the harrowing account of how government soldiers broke into her house when her parents were away looking for food and asked her where the rebels were hiding. When she denied any knowledge of the rebels, they beat her and her younger siblings and looted the house. When the younger children ran away, one of the soldiers cornered her sister and stripped off her clothes and was about to rape her when the wall of the house collapsed and the soldier had to run away. She escaped with only bruises, but many women and girls are not as fortunate and easily become victims of sexual assaults by both government soldiers and rebels.

Another woman was raped by many rebels right in front of her family. She still has nightmares that soldiers are coming to rape her again. A recent report on the refugee situation in South Sudan found a repeated occurrence of government forces unlawfully targeting civilians for murder, rape, torture, and destruction of property. Government soldiers target members of ethnic groups that are suspected of supporting the rebels, and the rebels target members of ethnic groups that support the government.

MINISTERING TO REFUGEE CHILDREN

As a trained social worker and with my past involvement in student ministries, I felt strongly about returning to my homeland to serve the South Sudanese people who are victims of political instability and forceful displacement. I sensed particularly called to minister to women, children, and youth. Earlier I had worked with college students as a missionary with Intervarsity Christian Fellowship, and after completing graduate studies abroad I was placed as a lecturer in the University of Juba in the capital city of South Sudan.

With the help of some friends, we began to conduct meetings for children and youth in nearby villages and towns. We met young people who had been traumatized by what had been done to them or by events taking places in the country. A large number of children are constantly on the move; after dropping out of school, they are now faced with the uncertainties and insecurities of a nomadic lifestyle. Having fled their hometowns, they have very little with them by the time they reach the southern part of the country. They are continually faced with life-threatening conditions and the risk of catching diseases.

At an international Christian mission conference in Jakarta, Indonesia, in 2016, I connected with other South Sudanese and Ugandan Christians who agreed to visit refugee camps with me and help conduct meetings for the refugee children in the Bidibidi (a small border village in northwestern Uganda) camp. Although most people have not heard of this refugee camp, with the rising tide of refugees from South Sudan and elsewhere it has become the largest refugee camp in the world—larger even than the Dadaab refugee camp in Kenya.

Our small team began visiting this camp and gathering children and youth living nearby. We created some activities for young children, as well as older teenagers, and began doing outreach in refugee camps. They were eager to come and be with our team and volunteers from the church. Our meetings provided music, Bible stories, and life-transforming testimonies. In light of the current situation in South Sudan, we decided to make forgiveness and reconciliation one of the major themes of our meetings. Many sought help from our team and just wanted to talk about what they were going through. Many shared their fears, losses, and abuses. One young mother confided in me that she decided to leave her village after her neighbors were locked in their home and burned alive. Though safe in Uganda, she is still fearful that something will happen to her three children.

A young boy gave his testimony after a children's meeting we held in his camp. He was staying with his uncle in the refugee camp, although his parents were also there. His uncle always mistreated him, and he was not allowed to go to church. But after attending our conference in the camp, he was overwhelmed with joy for the teaching of forgiveness and purity. On the last day of the conference, he shared about all the new things he learned and testified that he had forgiven his uncle, would try to live a pure life, and desired to grow up to be a good father in the future.

Another participant from the Bidibidi camp said, "Today, on behalf of my mother and all the family members, before God I have forgiven people for all the bad things they have done to us since we came to the refugee camp. Praise be to God for this conference, because I have gotten a chance to reconcile with my nephew, after one year, who sold our ration cards and disappeared from the family. The entire family suffered because of him, but today we are reconciling back as a family in the presence of God's people."

Another lady shared her story when her parents were accused of witchcraft in their village back in South Sudan and she was rejected by all her friends in school. She ended her story by saying, "Joseph's humility, perseverance, and patience has taught me to be calm toward accusations and only stick to Jesus as a model of my life and let God restore my hope in Christ."

At another refugee camp, we joined with the Scripture Union staff to conduct meetings for women and children. One of our volunteers shared his experiences: "At the Junior Scripture Union outreach programs, we taught several refugee communities how to live a pure life. I was convicted to share the gospel with refugees using 'Cross Talk.' I remember I was once a refugee like them, dressed like them, and scouting for food every day. I shared with them how I accepted Christ and the difference it made in my life. I told them how I became committed to my church and how important the new church family is to me. Once when I shared my testimony with a family of eight children, four of them accepted Christ. And one parent who was close to the venue appreciated our ministry and requested that we conduct similar programs for the elderly."

Another growing problem facing young children in the refugee camps is premature exposure to adult sexual content by watching pornography in video halls and on smartphones. We conducted small group discussions, where boys shared their lives with male teachers and girls shared separately with female teachers. Some boys freely talked about how they got exposed to pornography through their older brothers' smartphones. Several admitted that they were hoping to have sex with girls in the camp. However, as our volunteers taught about sexual abstinence, the children were challenged by the story of Joseph in the Bible. Many committed to sexual purity and gave their lives to Jesus. They also promised to be obedient and listen to their parents and teachers.

CONCLUSION

South Sudan is just like any other place in the world that is crying out for help arising out of mass displacement and a refugees crisis. It takes people with heart and passion to step up and get involved. Christian social workers often perceive a call not only to service in secular settings, but also to share their professional knowledge in congregational settings, particularly in their own faith communities by providing valuable information to faith communities about processes, procedures, and resources. I was able to gather critical information to assist churches in developing plans to minister to refugees. I was able to mobilize social work professionals to address refugee issues and train them to be teachers in the refugee camps. We empowered teachers and social workers to become advocates for refugees and bring about positive change on behalf of the powerless, voiceless, and disenfranchised refugees, particularly children.

The refugee problem is not a one person's responsibility nor can it be left to the government to resolve. The church, which is the body of Christ, has a great role to play. The Apostle Paul wrote about how believers must act toward others within the body of Christ and those who are outsiders: "Whatever you do, do it heartily, as to the Lord and not to men" (Col 3:23 NKJV). There is no way to serve God unless we serve his people by loving them. God's loves flows through us to people around us. Love comes from the heart, and our ministry must include those who are inside the church as well as reach those outside. We must get out of the comfort zones of our home and pews to reach the needy, hopeless, and less privileged among us. God desires the same standard from us and calls us to serve the least among us.

chapter fourteen

Compassion Fatigue: Never Grow Weary of Doing Good

Among the staff of the ministry of Heart for Lebanon, conversations switch very quickly from friends who hid refugee families in their home for two months to scrounging for food in the middle of a war zone. For our ministry team, both are part of normal life, daily routine, and regular work. War is never normal, however, and its aftermath is gruesome and unimaginable for most people. For our staff—and others who work with refugees in Lebanon and elsewhere— who are constantly steeped in the horrific effects of war on fellow human beings, it takes a toll. They love the people they work with, but giving so much of oneself is exhausting, especially when there is no end to the influx of refugees coming across the Syrian border. The demands far exceed the supply of our spiritual, emotional, and material capacity to serve. Some feel they are running on fumes, while others are sure to run out of fuel and come to a standstill soon.

What is compassion fatigue? Omri Elisha describes compassion fatigue as "the gaps between one's moral ambitions and the conditions of existence that reinforce and simultaneously threaten to undermine them at every turn."[275] More scientifically, in helping professions such as nursing, emergency care, and even public law, compassion fatigue is closely related to negative outcomes like depression, secondary trauma, and functional impairment—which have highly adverse effects on workers and organizations. Although there has been

---

1 I am grateful for the assistance of Haley Clasen and Amy Melki in conducting this research and helping to write this chapter.
2 Elisha, *Moral Ambition: Mobilization and Social Outreach in Evangelical Megachurches* (Berkeley, CA: University of
   California Press, 2011), 154.

little research on compassion fatigue related to humanitarian conditions, these situations are more likely to cause extreme stress and compassion fatigue.

SYRIAN REFUGEE CRISIS

Heart for Lebanon finds itself in the middle of a humanitarian crisis due to the influx of refugees fleeing conflict zones like Iraq and Syria. A small country of just over four thousand square miles and a population of 6.2 million people is faced with caring for over a million refugees fleeing for their dear lives. Situated next to the war zones, Lebanon has become a natural destination of the escaping refugees in the region; but without much assistance, the country is struggling to maintain any normalcy.

Although Lebanon is not the only neighboring country that has received large numbers of refugees, it hosts the largest number of refugees per capita. Simply put, one in every four people in Lebanon is a Syrian refugee. The larger country of Jordan, which also shares a border with Syria, has a ratio of one Syrian refugee for every ten people. And Turkey, to the north, hosts three million of the approximately six million Syrian refugees. Besides facing other internal problems, Lebanon's infrastructure, educational system, and health care—along with the sociopolitical will of the entire nation—has come under severe strain due to helping refugees from Syria.

In response to such needs, Heart for Lebanon seeks to restore hope to broken communities that have steadily increased in number across the border. Driven by the compassionate heart of Jesus Christ, Heart for Lebanon exists to see lives changed and communities transformed through a holistic approach. As we serve refugees, our ministries aim to provide these families with spiritual, social, emotional, and physical transformation. Whether through our monthly food portions, Bible studies, educational programs, or house visits, Christ is always at the center of what we do.

Figure 16: Dead or Missing Refugees Crossing the Mediterranean Sea (2014–17)

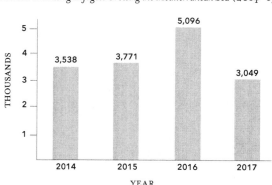

As our ministry team cries, laughs, and prays with families, it is impossible to escape the effects and emotional strain that result from the continuous encounter of horrific stories of war. For this reason we conducted a survey to study the presence or absence of compassion fatigue among our ministry team. Most research suggests that compassion fatigue is not, in and of itself, an issue; rather, compassion fatigue is a natural result of working in any helping profession. With high levels of compassion satisfaction or fulfillment in a helping profession, compassion fatigue is manageable and does not necessarily lead to burnout or other related issues.3 Given this, the real risk occurs among those who have both high compassion fatigue and low compassion satisfaction.

In June of 2017, the Heart for Lebanon team took the Compassion Fatigue and Satisfaction Self-Test, a survey examining levels of fatigue, satisfaction, and burnout. Over half of the Heart for Lebanon team had "high" or "extremely high" levels of compassion fatigue, which was initially disquieting. However, compassion satisfaction was so high that only 1 percent of respondents were classified "high risk," experiencing both low satisfaction and high fatigue. As a result, burnout scores were very low, with 86 percent of respondents at "extremely low" risk of burnout and the rest at only "moderate" risk. When compassion satisfaction is high, fatigue is less concerning, because staff members may "run out" but are also being refilled. This survey made us realize that ongoing support is required for staff in high-fatigue settings, especially if they are going to remain in the organization long-term, and that we had much room for growth in this area, especially for the 14 percent at "moderate" risk levels.

RETHINKING COMPASSION

The shift away from "compassion fatigue" to "compassion satisfaction" suggests a new mindset regarding what compassion really is, which is an essential issue for those seeking to follow Christ in not-for-profit work. Instead of looking narrowly at compassion as a finite resource, refugee ministries should aim to become "compassionate by character"—cultivating, as Chris Frakes says, "a disposition that does not mire them in anguish over the enormity and intractability of human suffering, but rather motivates them to perform actions aimed at the alleviation of such suffering."4

Jesus' compassionate character showed each time he looked over a crowd, had compassion on them, and began preaching or healing, pointing them back to the Father. Yet too often compassion is not understood as a sole virtue but is

---

3 Melissa Radey and Charles Figley, "The Social Psychology of Compassion," *Clinical Social Work Journal* 35, no. 3 (Fall 2007): 207–14.
4 Chris Frakes, "When Strangers Call: A Consideration of Care, Justice, and Compassion," *Hypatia* 25, no. 1 (Winter 2010): 93.

mixed with other values, leading to greater expectations of what compassion does—and to disappointment when the results are different.

Frakes outlines two other values that often coincide with compassion: care and justice. Care, she says, is concerned with the daily well-being and long-term goals of those close to us, whereas compassion meets strangers in their moment of need.[5] If we confuse compassion and care, we begin to believe compassion requires personal attention to all aspects of life for those we serve, rather than targeted intervention in moments of greatest need. Then we expect deep engagement with hundreds of people and become frustrated at the unsustainable nature of such an expectation.

Our strategy involves meeting physical needs (humanitarian relief) and relational engagement (one-on-one conversations) for spiritual discipleship, because Jesus loves and sees a whole person, not just an empty stomach. Our ministry team can meet strangers in their moment of need because they trust that families are supported in many facets of life, allowing team members to limit their responsibility to compassion, not care. In fact, when asked to choose between statements that defined compassion as care and compassion as compassion, over 80 percent of the team chose a definition of compassion distinct from care. Individual members do not have to carry the full lives of those they serve because the organization has a full support network built into its structure.

Justice aims to lift the oppressed and marginalized and, by definition, would not support the oppressor, the one who causes pain. Compassion, however, seeks to serve everyone in their moment of need, regardless of whether they are oppressed or oppressor.[6] For our ministry, this distinction is particularly acute due to the violent Syrian occupation of Lebanon during the Lebanese war (1975–90). Many team members hated Syrians and viewed them as oppressors, so when Syrian refugees began flooding Lebanon to escape their war, serving them was not an easy option. Yet Jesus is at work transforming hearts, and over 90 percent of our staff believe they need to show compassion to everyone, even oppressors. Today staff members enter the homes of Syrian refugees and say, "I used to hate Syrians because they occupied Lebanon. Yet Jesus has worked in my heart, and I am in your home today and want to serve you." Justice is not ignored, and the oppressed must be set free. But sometimes compassion can be the vehicle for that freedom.

Finally, Elisha outlines another conceptual distinction between compassion and accountability. Evangelicals in particular struggle to make this distinction.

---

5 Chris Frakes, "When Strangers Call: A Consideration of Care, Justice, and Compassion," *Hypatia* 25, no. 1 (Winter 2010): 93.

6 Ibid., 81–82.

Our biblical hermeneutic of a God who gives both unqualified grace and conditional covenants leaves us caught between "unconditional benevolence and reciprocal obligations," where we expect those we serve to reciprocate or respond to our aid, yet mask this expectation in a language of compassion.[7]

We take a different approach, however. Over 75 percent of the staff preferred the statement "Compassion does not depend on results" over "The person receiving it must change." In a particularly poignant example of this, a staff member visited a very conservative Muslim refugee family. Though the family allowed her to pray in Jesus' name, they whispered verses from the Qur'an under their breath and were extremely hostile to any conversation about Jesus. In debriefing the visit, the staff member made it very clear that her job was not to change them. She noted that God may be working in ways we don't see and that she will continue to pray with them and for them in Jesus' name. Her focus was not on the result but on the process, allowing her to continue showing compassion. While we hope for change on the part of those we serve, that is not our job. Only God can work and transform people's hearts.

A fuller definition of compassion, distinct from care, justice, and accountability, allows those who work with refugees to become increasingly "compassionate by character." As compassion becomes part of who we are, we become less and less worried about "running out." Compassion fatigue can be replaced with compassion satisfaction when we no longer expect it to also involve supporting every need, overturning oppression, or seeing the results that care, justice, and accountability would lead us to expect. When we live with the virtue of compassion, we can, like Jesus, look over crowds of refugees we wish we could serve and, as one of our cofounder says, "Do for one what we wish we could do for everyone."

STRATEGIES TO INCREASE COMPASSION SATISFACTION

To keep the team healthy, our ministry aims to sustain and increase compassion satisfaction through a few different strategies, such as spiritual retreats, monthly "family day," "fun day" outings, and spontaneous group activities. Not all strategies have worked well, and some have been successful only at specific periods of time over the last ten years. Being a young organization, we are trying to sustain compassion satisfaction and deal with compassion fatigue among our staff.

Other proven strategies to increase compassion satisfaction include the development of dynamic leadership that emphasizes the emotional, rather

---

7 Elisha, *Moral Ambition*, 155–57.

than technical, aspects of leadership. Dynamic leaders focus on supporting and challenging employees to do their jobs well rather than detailing exact methods, thus fostering relationships of trust both between leader and employee and between fellow employees.[8]Another way is to spend time directly with refugees. Our study found that those who spent ten to forty hours per week with refugees had a much higher rate of compassion satisfaction than those who worked less than ten hours or more than forty hours. Studies have shown that those with higher levels of spirituality and religious involvement showed active coping strategies like reframing and emotional support.[9] Another proven strategy is building into employees' inner "compassionate core," which "consists of an individual's inner resources and capacities (i.e., thriving and resilience) and accumulated wisdom derived from life experiences."[10] This core drives helpers to helping professions and sustains them through tough times. We also attempt to create space for feelings of belonging to a community, which allows workers to increase compassion satisfaction.

When our team ranked which activities helped them feel most satisfied with their work, there was a direct match between the research above and our strategies. When we asked our team to rank their preferred strategies to increase compassion satisfaction, the highest-ranking result, interestingly, was "Having a positive relationship with your supervisor." Spiritual retreats and personal time off ranked second and third. Other strategies include regular debriefing with coworkers, family day, spontaneous group activities like watching football matches, and other fun activities. Another strategy is for staff to talk with the pastor in residence or personal mentors on a regular basis. As our team grows larger, we have to be more creative about the monthly family day for coming together to worship, pray, eat, and play. The importance of family days and retreats lies in the opportunity for our staff to wind down and reflect on the struggles and personal challenges that come with humanitarian work.

With these strategies, we hope to draw people together to support each other through ministry difficulties and to point people to the God who replenishes us daily with a compassion distinct from care, justice, and accountability.

---

8 Meredith A Newman, Mary E. Guy, and Sharon H. Mastracci. "Beyond Cognition: Affective Leadership and Emotional Labor," *Public Administration Review* 69, no. 1 (January–February 2009): 14.
9 Christian U. Krägeloh, Penny Pei Minn Chai, Daniel Shepherd, and Rex Billington, "How Religious Coping is Used Relative to Other Coping Strategies Depends on the Individual's Level of Religiosity and Spirituality," *Journal of Religion and Health* 51, no. 4 (December 2012): 1146.
10 Melissa Radey and Charles Figley, "The Social Psychology of Compassion," *Clinical Social Work Journal* 35, no. 3 (Fall 2007): 209.

CONCLUSION

It is only natural for people to be overwhelmed by caring for people fleeing war zones and to sense feelings of fatigue, exhaustion, and helplessness. However, the Apostle Paul, in his letter to the Galatians, exhorts, "Let us not grow weary of doing good," and concludes with a promise that "in due season we will reap, if we do not give up" (Gal 6:9 ESV). When inundated with needs far beyond our human or organizational capacity, it is easy to give up. Hence, our ministry leaders reviewed our staff policies about care for the caregivers and practical strategies to increase compassion satisfaction in the face of unending refugee influx and compassion fatigue.

chapter fifteen

*Staying for Good: Middle Eastern Christians
and the Challenge to Remain*

STEPHEN CARTER

Ibrahim[1] is a follower of Christ from a very conservative country on the Arabian Peninsula. As a convert from Islam, he faced a range of significant threats in his country. He was ostracized and threatened by close relatives, who were angry that their family name had been shamed and were determined to restore their honor by expunging the source of that shame. Ibrahim was unable to keep a job, being let go when rumors spread about his faith. And he dreaded the reaction of the authorities if those who knew his secret were to report him as an "apostate." According to Islamic law, apostasy is a capital offense.

Understandably, Ibrahim's fear and despair led him to make plans to leave. He longed for a place where he could worship the Lord freely, and he felt sure that the answer to his yearnings was Europe. By a variety of means, only some of them legal, Ibrahim traveled to a Western European country and claimed asylum. But he was taken back by the unexpected struggles and vulnerabilities he faced. The climate, culture, and language were disorientating; he felt isolated and unaccepted; the asylum process was long and confusing; he had no prospect of finding work. He was required to live in an immigration center alongside many Muslim asylum seekers, which made him wonder if he was in a better place after all. Even the church he found, though friendly, was largely inaccessible to a stranger. Ibrahim longed for his home country.

---

1 Name and some details altered to preserve anonymity.

Jean-Clément Jeanbart, Melkite Greek Catholic Archbishop of Aleppo, echoed views expressed by many other Syrian church leaders in an appeal in August of 2016:

> We believe that the Church must continue to live in this country where it has been founded. The Church began in Syria and should continue living in Syria until the coming back of the Lord. . . . As a pastor, as a recent successor of the apostles, I have this responsibility to help the people of the world to understand that. That we may fight, we may resist in order to remain where the Church was born. We do whatever we can to continue this presence, and we need you to help us remain where we are—to continue the life of Jesus Christ, of the Church, in this land.[2]

REFUGEE, CHRISTIAN, AND PERSECUTED

Ibrahim is a refugee, having fled persecution because of his Christian faith. Among the millions of displaced Syrians are many Christians, some of whom have fled religious persecution. They are part of the massive people movements of today—migrants and refugees, often desperate, traumatized and fearful, and yearning for dignity, identity, and safety in foreign lands.

Christian refugees, and more particularly those Christians who have fled religious-based persecution, may be a small proportion of today's massive people movements. But the global church arguably has a special responsibility for this category of refugees. As a church, we are one body, called to suffer alongside those parts of the body that suffer and to share the joy of those parts that are honored (1 Cor 12:26). The worldwide Christian community has the responsibility to care for all, not just for our own kind. As Catholic commentator John L. Allen puts it: "Should it be acceptable for Christians to feel a special, gut-level empathy for other Christians, because their faith says they're fellow members of the Body of Christ? Once more, of course."[3]

THE MIDDLE EASTERN CHURCH AND EMIGRATION

Much crucial theological and missiological reflection on people movements has focused on the impact, challenges, and opportunities for refugees and for receiving communities, whether in receiving countries or in transit points

---

2 Interview with Gretchen R. Crowe, *Our Sunday Visitor*, August 15, 2016, https://www.osv.com/Article/TabId/493/ArtMID/13569/ArticleID/20497/Aleppo-archbishop-Enough-is-enough.aspx (accessed October 1, 2017).

3 John L. Allen Jr., "Why Do Christians Hesitate to Rise Up on Anti-Christian Persecution?" Crux, August 18, 2017, https://cruxnow.com/analysis/2017/08/18/christians-hesitate-rise-anti-christian-persecution/ (accessed October 1, 2017).

along the way. In many places the slumbering church is becoming alert to the opportunity of compassionate engagement as a practical witness of Christ's love to refugees and is joining, in his name, with others of goodwill to counter the ugly reactions of the hateful and hurtful. At the same time, there has been a flurry of well-intentioned initiatives to support and encourage Christians who have been forced to flee because of persecution.

But might the focus on supporting migrants and refugees present a blind spot when it comes to the church? Is there a danger that we overlook the Christian communities in refugees' countries of origin? If we care about the future of the church in a region such as the Middle East, it is vital that we understand the impact of emigration out of this region. Yes, we long to see thriving communities of Arab believers in the European and North American cities to which refugees have fled—but we also long to see thriving communities of Arab believers in their own lands!

Emigration is not a new phenomenon for the Christian communities of the Middle East. For decades, indigenous Christian communities have dwindled as a proportion of the overall population.[4] This is the result of both demographic and economic factors: Christian families are typically smaller than Muslim families, and Christians have often had greater means to pursue further education or employment elsewhere in the world. A factor underlying the economic emigration-driver in recent decades has been religious-based discrimination. Legal, social, and religious obstacles faced by Christians (and other non-Muslim communities) have often limited the economic prospects of such groups. These pressures have intensified in recent years, particularly as extremist groups such as *Daesh* (the so-called "Islamic State") have sought to forcibly impose their brutal interpretations of Islam.

Although the persecution of Christians and some other religious communities in countries such as Iraq and Syria has been horrific, it is important to note that not all Christians who have fled from the Middle East in recent years have been directly threatened because of their faith. In fact, within refugee movements from the Middle East region in recent years there is little to suggest that Christians are disproportionately represented. Most Christians fleeing Syria, for example, have done so for the same reasons as their non-Christian compatriots—to escape the horrors of war, to pursue economic opportunity, to give their children a better future, to avoid military conscription, and to reignite a sense of hope for their future.

---

4 Todd Johnson of the Center for the Study of Global Christianity at Gordon-Conwell Theological Seminary estimates that in 1910 Christians accounted for 13.6 percent of the Middle East's population, by 2010 it had fallen to 4.2 percent, and that by 2025 it could be just over 3 percent. See https://www.wsj.com/articles/christians-in-an-epochal-shift-are-leaving-the-middle-east-1494597848 (accessed October 1, 2017).

The dynamics for the likes of Ibrahim, a convert from a Muslim background, are different than those for indigenous Christian communities. As the number of converts to Christianity in the region increases, a growing phenomenon has been the flight of converts escaping individual persecution, often at the hands of families or communities and Islamic radicals. These are often isolated individuals and families who remain vulnerable on the journey as they seek a place of safety. Family threats and government hostility toward Christian converts often continue even in transit locations abroad.

HELPING OR HINDERING?

In 2011, ministry leaders in the Religious Liberty Partnership[5] recognized a contradiction. On the one hand, Christians facing religious persecution, together with some outside agencies supporting them, were often quick to assume that relocation or extraction is the most appropriate response. On the other hand, there was a strong consensus among church leaders in countries where the church is under pressure that Christians should remain in their countries if possible, and that in the long run a hasty relocation can be problematic for the individuals, families, and communities involved.

To address this tension, members of the Religious Liberty Partnership established a policy whereby they would advise and assist Christians under persecution to relocate out of their country or region only as a matter of last resort, when no other viable options are available.[6] The rationale behind that policy, driven by the interests of local churches in the Middle East, is just as valid and vital today as it was in 2011 when the Syrian crisis had hardly begun. And it is a policy that I suggest should inform our missional engagement in whichever part of the world we live and in whatever capacity we serve.

The theological foundations of a policy to encourage Christians to remain in their countries whenever possible are broad. To flee persecution can certainly be a valid, biblical response to danger (Acts 9:23–25). But it can be equally valid to endure persecution with joy, counting it a privilege (Acts 5:41; 2 Tim 3:10–13; Jas 1:2), or to resist unjust treatment by claiming citizenship rights (Acts 22:25–29). Jesus established persecution as normative for his followers (John 15:20)—and yet how readily do we go out of our way to avoid danger at all costs? For some of us, does the risk aversion of our culture become an impediment to trusting God and faithfully obeying Christ? Are we too quick to project that risk aversion on others of different cultures?

5 A collaborative initiative nurturing partnering among Christian organizations focused on religious liberty. See www.rlpartnership.org.

6 See full policy statement and commitment: https://rlpartnership.org/wp-content/uploads/2017/10/RLP-Relocation-Policy-Statement-2017.pdf (accessed August 29, 2018).

Several scholars have developed a "theology of presence," including in light of recent dynamics in the Middle East. To understand the importance of Christian presence in Syria is to understand the prophetic role of the church and the calling of Christ's people as agents of reconciliation and transformation. It is to understand the imperative of maintaining a witness to the love, hope, peace, and life of Christ in a context of hatred, hopelessness, conflict, and death, and to understand how vital it is for the salt and light of Christ's people to permeate and help shape a post-conflict Syria.

If we are hasty in advising or assisting persecuted Christians to relocate, especially to Western countries, we can inadvertently send a signal that the destination countries are in some way superior to the countries of origin. Although that might hold true on the immediate issue of safety, the wider ramifications are dangerous and unhelpful, especially within the global church. A practical downside is that such approaches can encourage spurious claims of religious persecution among those who may primarily be attracted by the lure of opportunity and the material benefit they perceive elsewhere.

BUILDING HEALTHY CHURCHES

Getting the theology right as we respond to persecution is vital not just for the individuals involved but for the wider church, including the integrity of the church's witness. By encouraging and facilitating persecuted Christians to remain in their countries we foster the building up, not the depletion, of national churches in a region like the Middle East, whether long-standing indigenous churches or fledgling fellowships of new believers. It is for this reason that Archbishop Jeanbart is so adamant that Christians should stay in or return to Aleppo—Christ's people are vital witnesses.

For the emerging communities of believers from non-Christian backgrounds, the cycle of conversion-persecution-relocation must be broken if these communities are to flourish. When a believer flees from an abusive family, the relationship with the family is usually, at that point, irretrievably broken and the opportunity to bear faithful witness, however hard, is gone forever. Families and friends are unlikely to be convinced of the relevance of a faith that divides and alienates family members.

Relocation outside the region, especially if through asylum or refugee systems, is usually a long-term or permanent move. Even though some express a desire to return to their countries when the security situation allows, or when they are encouraged to do so, experience shows that very few, in fact, do so.

Typically, viable in-country or in-region options leave open the possibility of return. By leaving open the option of return for as long as it may take, we offer to persecuted Christians the prospect for forgiveness and reconciliation with perpetrators, for the encouragement and strengthening of the local church, and for positive impact within their societies and nations through the presence and witness of the church.

Christian communities under pressure, and organizations supporting them, often call for their rights to be recognized through appeals to human rights norms which hold that freedom of religion is a fundamental freedom that should be afforded to all.[7] To make such appeals is to recognize the importance of pluralistic systems of governance that provide for religious and other freedoms. The indigenous Christian communities of the Middle East are an integral part of their societies, having contributed significantly to the rich heritage of their countries since the earliest days of the church. Political leaders such as King Abdullah II of Jordan have recognized the contributions of Christians and have affirmed the importance of maintaining a Christian presence in the region, which enriches and promotes cohesion in their societies.[8] So to encourage or facilitate the emigration of Christians from the Middle East is to undermine those efforts to preserve and promote pluralism.

Asylum, refugee, and resettlement systems have long been time-consuming and challenging processes, with a high burden of proof on applicants, prolonged periods of uncertainty while decisions are awaited (sometimes in conditions where maintaining dignity is a challenge), and significant rates of non-acceptance. As the global movement of people has spiked, host countries and agencies such as the UNHCR have become overwhelmed. It is common for those embarking on these processes to have unrealistic expectations—which then compound the frustration when faced with reality. So even if a Christian has strong documentary evidence of religiously motivated persecution, the practical issues presented by refugee systems reinforce the view that it be used only as a last resort.

And many of those who do reach a place of safety find, like Ibrahim, that their new country is not the utopia they dreamed of. In addition to the challenge of physical and cultural adjustments, Christian refugees have expressed shock at the "godlessness" of Western countries, new temptations, and even the struggle to adapt to different church environments. Anecdotal

---

7 Article 18 of the Universal Declaration of Human Rights (1948) establishes the right to hold a religion or belief of one's choice, and to practice a religion of one's choosing alone or with others in private or public.

8 King Abdullah asserted, "Arab Christians are an integral part of my region's past, present, future." "King Abdullah II on Condemning Religious Violence," Berkley Center for Religion, Peace, and World Affairs, September 24, 2014, https://berkleycenter.georgetown.edu/quotes/king-abdullah-ii-on-condemning-religious-violence (accessed October 1, 2017)

evidence suggests that a majority of Middle Eastern Christians from non-Christian backgrounds who flee from persecution by relocating to the "the West" end up losing their faith in their new location. If in our eagerness to help a persecuted sister or brother we naïvely increase the chances that they will fall away from the faith, are we really helping?

A WAY FORWARD

By outlining some of the many areas of challenges in regard to persecuted Christians fleeing to other countries, no criticism is meant of those who do flee or who provide vital support to refugees. The severity of persecution, and the limited extent of other durable solutions, means that there are inevitably many who do have to rely on these systems. And many have made successful adjustments and are thriving in new locations. However, those serving persecuted Christians must do so with their eyes open to the challenges, and in particular must strive to understand and respect the needs and priorities of churches in countries of origin.

For that reason, members of the Religious Liberty Partnership also made a series of commitments for the handling of cases of potential relocation of persecuted Christians. One commitment was to seek advice and authorization from local church and ministry leaders and to take account of implications for wider communities and the church and not just the individuals involved. Another commitment was to consider in-country and in-region relocation options before pursuing out-of-region options. Local options, when available, are typically more straightforward logistically, can be implemented more rapidly, are less costly financially, and involve less cultural adjustment than out-of-region relocation.

A further commitment was to collaborate with others, including local partners, to meet the many support needs of those facing persecution, whether they remain within their communities or are forced to relocate. Such partnership and cooperation can open a greater range of options, such as temporary study or employment opportunities in nearby countries. The extensive list of support needs that arise for individuals and their families—including spiritual, emotional/psychological, financial, medical, logistical, educational, and occupational—can sometimes be met more fully or adequately closer to home than out of the region.

These commitments are a step in the right direction, and we rejoice in the progress made in recent years. The Middle Eastern church will clearly continue to need support, encouragement, and prayer in the coming years. Perhaps agencies responding to emergency situations are reluctant to commit to coordination and collaboration because it could slow our responses. But then again, perhaps if greater care had been taken to advise and support Ibrahim appropriately, he might not have faced such disillusionment. As we bear witness to Christ and to his people in the region, the challenge for us all is to take seriously the appeal of Archbishop Jeanbart—to help Christians stay for good.

chapter sixteen

Young Refugees: Building Leaders for Peace

SAJI OOMMEN

Birthed in Turkey, Building Leaders for Peace (BL4P) is a new movement that envisions a peaceful future by partnering with and equipping young people in conflict regions around the world. BL4P intends to create a movement of people who recognize their shared humanity regardless of age, race, or religion, who are developing a lifestyle of peace, and who are committed to being peace leaders in their communities.

In this chapter I will share the five key values of BL4P and illustrate them with stories that demonstrate the impact of this movement on the lives of young refugees from Syria and Iraq, preparing them for a hopeful and peaceful future.

BL4P VALUE #1: IDENTITY AND STORY

We all belong to a narrative, a story that informs who we are, where we come from, and what we stand for. At BL4P, we believe in sharing our stories with one another and writing new chapters together. We are passionate about stories that acknowledge our common humanity and compel us toward a future of peace.

With tears streaming down her face, Alma (not her real name), a Syrian refugee living in southeastern Turkey, walked up to the front of the group at our peace camp, looked at the audience, and said, "I want to forgive the pilot who dropped a bomb and killed my father."

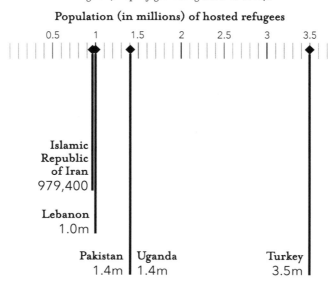

Figure 17: Top Refugee-hosting Countries (2017)

This was a powerful moment at the peace camp we hosted in August 2016. Alma had just shared a slideshow of photos of her father and explained how he had been killed two years earlier in Aleppo. This had sent her into a downward spiral of anger and bitterness. When she arrived at the camp, she told everyone on the first day that maybe Allah would forgive the pilot, but she wouldn't. Alma admitted that she received strength to forgive from being with this group of people at BL4P, people whom she now calls family. Her story compelled us toward a future of peace.

Alma and her husband, Mahfuz (not his real name), are Syrian refugees living in Turkey. They were part of a group of sixty Syrians and ten Turks that came together with about thirty Americans and Canadians to talk about peace. Alma listened to other people talk about reconciliation and engaged in the games and activities that reinforced the themes and the spirit of community.

The day before, Alma had watched another Syrian refugee walk up front and share with the camp participants about the racism and prejudice he had experienced from Turks since coming to Turkey. These experiences had made him bitter and angry, and he had in turn begun to be prejudiced toward Turks and express racist statements toward them. He asked for forgiveness from the Turks. Upon hearing this, two young Turkish men in the audience walked forward and hugged him. This was a wonderful expression of reconciliation and another powerful story of peace.

At these week-long camps, participants are immersed in intentional multicultural community, cross-cultural collaboration, perspective sharing, and service projects. The first five days of the peace camp are focused on the themes of celebrating diversity, collaboration, conflict transformation, catalytic leadership through forgiveness and reconciliation, and changing the world. The last two days are spent in service activities that bring together the ideas that have been discussed and put them into practical application. Thus participants internalize values of peacebuilding through learning and activities within a loving and hopeful community.

BL4P VALUE #2: FORGIVENESS AND RECONCILIATION

Change begins within ourselves. As we experience the power of forgiveness in our own hearts, we see how this peace affects our relationships with others. We believe that any conflict, whether big or small, can be overcome through love and forgiveness. At BL4P, we strive to provide spaces where differences can be understood and opponents can be reconciled, so we can truly experience peace and unity.

During one of our small group times after the theme of forgiveness, Mahfuz shared that he could never forgive the people who had imprisoned him. He then got up and shared with the whole group what had happened to him. One of the North American participants wrote about what happened next:

Mahfuz had just shared about his experiences in a Syrian prison. He was looking right at Alma, revealing details of his torture that he had never shared with her because she had already experienced enough pain and grief over the bombing death of her father. In the safety of that multicultural family, Mahfuz quietly told the jarring reality of torture with water and electric probes. Mahfuz admitted he didn't know how he could forgive, but in his admission, I sensed that there was a plea for freedom from his anger and hatred toward his aggressors.

As people were leaving the building, we stayed back, and I told him of my own experience in Colombia with injustice and violence by aggressive, angry men. I acknowledged that these experiences now had become part of our life stories, and the physical and emotional reminders could either become festering, bitter wounds or healed scars. The difference between a wound and a scar was my choice for bondage or freedom. Unforgiveness was a road to bondage and forgiveness was our road to freedom. I shared with Mahfuz that forgiving those men had set my heart and mind on a road free of bitterness, hatred, and fear. Those three enemies would steal our peace, so we needed to daily choose to forgive in order to be freed from their binding chains. Mahfuz thanked me for sharing my story, allowed me to pray for him, and said he would really think about this idea of freedom through forgiveness.

The next day he and Alma came to me and Mahfuz calmly thanked me again and said that he had made the choice to forgive his enemies. As many times as he would need to, he would continue to forgive them so he could live with freedom from fear, bitterness, and hatred. He was at peace with this choice. At our Peace Camp, Mahfuz found a space where he could grapple with the reality of forgiveness and reconciliation. A change began within his heart and he decided to let go of his negative feelings and receive peace.

BL4P VALUE #3: COMMUNITY

At BL4P, we see community as the building block for peace, a safe place in which we are encouraged to ask questions, to find common ground, to challenge one another's ideologies, and to learn from one another.

Despite our differences, we need one another, and so we need to learn how to be together in ways that show honesty, respect, and humility. The Contact Theory developed by Greg Allport in the 1950s was used by Brenda McNeil for her reconciliation work:

Relationships between conflicting groups will improve if they have meaningful contact over an extended period of time. This contact must occur in a mutually beneficial learning environment and involve multiple opportunities for participants to have cooperative interactions with one another. According to the theory, this type of contact will likely decrease the hostility between groups because the animosity is typically fueled by stereotypes that result from limited exposure.[1]

Contact theory explains some of the understanding of community that we have developed at our peace camps. We want to create these safe spaces where people can come together to talk about peace and reconciliation. These are not Christian camps or Muslim camps, but rather spaces where people from different ethnicities and cultures come into contact with each other and shake off the media-driven misunderstandings that we have of each other and begin to embrace each other as we really are. These safe spaces are containers that we create for the Spirit to move and shape the circumstances and to transform the people.

---

[1] Brenda Salter McNeil, *Roadmap to Reconciliation: Moving Communities into Unity, Wholeness and Justice* (Downers Grove, IL: IVP Books, 2015), 33.

In 2017, we held a peace camp in Iraq with Yazidis, Iraqi Arabs, and Kurds, as well as North Americans. Hakim (not his real name) was an Iraqi Muslim whose sisters had come to our peace camp in 2016 and encouraged him to come to the camp in 2017. He came to Turkey and had a powerful time in this experiential learning community. When he heard that we were putting on a camp in Iraq, he decided that he wanted to come because this was his land.

During one of our sessions, we had a time when we gathered the Yazidis in a circle and began to pray for them and for what they had experienced over the course of the last several years: being persecuted by radicals, fleeing from their homes in Sinjar, and now living in refugee camps in northern Iraq. Hakim was deeply moved and stepped into the circle to share. He looked at the Yazidi people and told them that, as an Iraqi Muslim, he needed to apologize to them for the persecution they had experienced from his people and ask for their forgiveness. Immediately, one of the Yazidis came forward and gave him a deep embrace and forgave him.

BL4P VALUE #4: LEADERSHIP

A leader is someone who demonstrates what is possible, and more specifically at BL4P, that peace is possible. As leaders of peace, we believe that everyone can be a peacemaker, so we boldly invite others into the peacemaking process. But before mobilizing others, we must first model peace in our own lives.

In August of 2017, we held our second BL4P peace camp in Turkey. Alma and Mahfuz attended the gathering with their six-month-old daughter. They wanted to continue to be a part of this growing movement because they wanted to create a future of peace for their daughter. When Alma was invited to share her experiences of the last camp, she readily agreed. She talked about the hate and anger she had felt, but then she shared about three different participants at the last camp who prayed for her and encouraged her. She shared her story so that it would encourage others to forgive and to begin a process of healing in their own lives and the lives of others.

We want to build leaders of peace for the future—young leaders who understand what it takes emotionally, spiritually, and physically and are prepared to take risks for a movement of peace. These are men and women who have learned how to forgive, who pursue hope amid the hard circumstances of life and want to impact their community in small and large ways. Ultimately, we believe that transformed people can transform their communities.

Near the end of our second camp in Turkey, we gave out the "5M" awards to five young people who exhibited strong leadership potential. The awards were based on the examples of five peace leaders who have impacted the world in powerful ways: Martin Luther King, Malala Yousafzai, Mother Teresa, Mahatma Gandhi, and Nelson Mandela. We wanted to make sure that our community could learn from these peacemaking giants.

BL4P VALUE #5: COLLABORATION

Creating a community of peace is just the beginning. It requires respect for one another as well as a willingness to learn from one another's experiences and ideas that will move us to make a difference. At BL4P, we use creative and interactive activities to encourage each participant to contribute what they know and what they envision for their community as we seek to understand peace and find ways to move toward it.

Over the past two years Alma and Mahfuz have become a part of the BL4P movement. After the first camp, they helped start a BL4P chapter in their community. A chapter is a group of people who want to continue the process started at a camp and see it expressed in their homes and community. More than six chapters have started in Turkey, and chapters have begun to form in Iraq.

These chapters become the seedbed for training and leadership development. On their own initiative, participants in Turkey began to brainstorm ways to impact their community. The hashtag *#peace is possible* became a rallying cry for these young people as they passed out flowers and candy during Eid, a Muslim celebration springing from Abraham's sacrifice. They visited nursing homes and orphanages, bringing cheer and care to the neediest of society.

Now Mahfuz and Alma are part of a community-development corporation started by Syrians to meet the needs of Syrian refugees. They are engaged in making a difference in their community for themselves and for their one-year-old daughter and others. As Alma closed her talk to the peace camp participants, she said, "I want everyone to feel this freedom, because hate is really heavy on your heart."

If you are interested in starting a BL4P peace camp or you would like more information, please go to our website at bl4p.com.

chapter seventeen

Refugees and Technology:
Leveraging Modern Tools for Safe Passage

Abdulla had escaped from the war zone of northern Damascus in Syria and was now sailing on a rubber boat that had launched from the western coast of Turkey. As the shoreline of the Greek island of Lesbos came closer, the sixteen-year-old had only one thing on his mind. He wasn't concerned about finding food or seeking shelter for the night when he reached the island, but rather about how to get a smartphone! Sure enough, upon landing on the island beach Abdulla borrowed a phone from a stranger to call his brother in Germany, and within minutes his brother arranged to send him some money. The first thing the young refugee bought with the money, of course, was his own phone.

Modern communication and internet technologies have come to the aid of refugees in unbelievable ways, becoming indispensable tools for finding safe passages and for sheer survival. These technologies provide refugees with the latest information, emotional support for scattered family members and friends, and the means to secure financial assistance amid the uncertainties of nomadic life. They deliver the latest news flashes about ever-changing policies regarding refugee pathways, weather reports, security alerts, videos, and even entertainment along the perilous journey. Refugees depend on mobile financial services for cash transfers and to send remittance back home. A smartphone's camera, digital storage, apps, and Wi-Fi access empower refugees unlike anything else in the course of their wanderings.

If not for these gadgets and connectivity, many refugees would have perished during their journeys. Having current and accurate information at their fingertips is a lifesaving asset on their dangerous treks across deserts and seas. Last summer, a boat carrying twenty-five refugees was sinking in the Mediterranean Sea off the Spanish coast when one of the passengers managed to send an SOS message, with their precise location on WhatsApp. The Spanish coast guard arrived and rescued them all.

However, the same technologies are also being used by human traffickers and others to entice innocent refugee victims and exploit their human predicament. Corrupt officials rely on the same tools, apps, and social media content to exploit people along the refugee corridors for financial extortion or abuse. Many young people from war-ravaged countries are allured and raped by smugglers and forced into prostitution. Some online groups take advantage of desperate refugees by recruiting them into radical terrorist groups, while other refugees have paid dearly for misinformation and fake news on the web. Technological ignorance has negatively impacted some refugees, particularly women and those who are older.

TECHNOLOGY AIDING REFUGEE COMMUNITIES

Access to information is clearly empowering to refugees as they navigate the convoluted quagmires of refugee highways. Realizing that smartphones have proven to be a critical lifeline for refugees, many aid workers, agencies, and volunteers are providing innovative services and solutions for this unexpected new market segment. Mobile tools are also critical for refugees' livelihood and integration in host societies, as they help them find jobs, learn new languages, obtain emergency help, maintain connections, and manage their finances. Some have even started businesses such as mobile repair services to address the needs of refugee communities by leveraging technology tools and platforms. The massive and sudden surge in refugee movements through the Eastern Mediterranean route to Greece in 2015 was aided by strong connectivity and smartphones. The tragedies along the route also spread like wildfire, alerting others along the way.

Humanitarian agencies and tech companies have realized the unexpected, widespread usage of modern technology tools and are joining hands with nonprofits and intergovernmental agencies to develop refugee-specific apps. UNICEF's family tracing and reunification is an open-source mobile application that helps children reunite with their parents or other caregivers. Google Maps, WhatsApp, YouTube, Viber, Facebook, and other social media sites help refugees stay connected with family members and other refugees who are in different places along the most massive forceful displacement of people in human history. A few Silicon Valley companies have partnered with a leading nonprofit refugee agency to develop Refugee.Info, an online platform and app that delivers up-to-date information to asylum-seekers. REFUNITE is a platform supported by Ericsson and several agencies, including the Red Cross, which is helping separated refugee families reconnect. Numerous groups and forums on Facebook, WeChat, and other social media sites are specifically geared toward refugees' movement in different countries. Others have used the latest 3D printing technology for prosthetics, which are inexpensive and custom-built, and echo location devices that allow the visually impaired to navigate their homes.

Many national telecom operators in Europe are helping meet essential connectivity needs and Wi-Fi hotspots for refugees. Vodafone provides instant connectivity and recharging stations to refugees arriving on the shores of Greece. Deutsche Telekom's website careers4refugees.de helps recently arrived refugees find jobs and other essential services in Germany. Hello Hope, a language-translation app developed by Turkcell for Syrian refugees arriving in Turkey, has had nearly a million users in a little over a year. Many government agencies in Europe are leveraging data tools and information about refugees for surveillance and to proactively detect any potential security concerns.

Red Cross and Red Crescent societies across Europe have established a family-finding initiative called Trace the Face, which publishes photos of separated or missing individuals online so that their relatives can search for them using various filtering criteria, like gender, age, and originating province or country. They are hoping to integrate artificial intelligence and facial-recognition technology to help refugees and their families find each other, even when they are scattered over a large geographical region. When it is difficult to establish the legal identity of refugees in a foreign country, the latest tools—biometrics, iris scans, fingerprints, and photographs collected at different transit points along the refugee routes—have proven not only to be invaluable resources but a smart way to manage large numbers of constantly moving people without proper legal documentation.

Some estimate that as many as 80 percent of refugees in Europe have smartphones. Information provided through those phones can have incredible reach and impact in serving refugees everywhere. Most refugees who make it to Europe are young and savvy to use modern technology tools to organize, communicate, and mobilize resources. The elderly, women, less educated, technology illiterate, and rural folks are disadvantaged in their access to information, technology, and connectivity. This digital divide is very consequential for refugees, who often turn to younger refugee sojourners, even children, to use the modern gadgets. Some young refugee computer programmers have developed apps based on their own distinct vantage point regarding the services sought in destination countries and are selling these tools to host-nation corporations or telecom companies.

Developmental platforms such as MIT's App Inventor are turning young refugees into software developers, and some very creative smartphone apps have been developed, which solve their own problems with the aid of some of the most advanced tools that Silicon Valley entrepreneurs could have ever envisioned. Refugees use apps to secure emergency medical diagnoses from doctors and hospitals remotely, while authorities keep track of any outbreak of disease in the refugee camps. The social enterprise Techfugees hosted a hackathon in Jordan that brought young technologists and entrepreneurs together to collaborate and develop new solutions to problems in refugee camps. The contest was won by two female refugees who used crowdsourcing to identify water leakages in water distribution, educate people about water conservation, and address the problem of water shortages.

Numerous information and communications technology (ICT) based projects, such as ReBootKAMP, train refugees in advanced software skills and open many doors for acquiring employment and building self-confidence in a foreign land. Refugee Open Ware (ROW) creates opportunities for refugees from conflict-affected regions to leverage computing and communication technologies by providing the latest gadgets, tools, training, support, and startup ecosystems. The possibilities for how one could use technology to serve refugees are truly endless.

REFUGEE MINISTRIES USING TECHNOLOGY

Utilizing technology tools has become a significant ministry strategy for many Christian refugee organizations and services. They use the latest tools to offer practical services as well as to engage in spiritual matters. Displacement and wanderings deepen people's spiritual quest, and also cause them to question some of the belief systems they grew up with. Refugees show great openness to new ideas and feel empowered to choose for themselves in foreign lands. They search for and listen to Christian messages and programs on the internet, as more Christian content is being streamed along refugee pathways and settlements.

A few Christian ministries that are involved in reaching and ministering to refugees in Europe have recognized the enormous potential of technology tools in connecting with and serving today's refugees. Christian websites using the Arabic, Farsi, and Pashtun languages are receiving substantial visitors from refugee hotspots in Turkey, Jordan, Lebanon, Greece, Italy, Austria, Germany, and beyond. Demands for Arabic Bibles and literature in Europe are growing, as many churches and ministries are involved in distributing them to refugees. Many access them online and also join online forums or chat with virtual pastors and counselors.

World Vision, with help from Microsoft, developed the #NoLostGeneration initiative to create technology-based educational solutions for Syrian children. Christian humanitarian and settlement agencies leverage technology tools extensively to reach and minister to refugees. Christian trauma counselors have developed material and offer their services freely to refugees at remote locations. The "JESUS" film is widely popular, and some evangelists have offered free Wi-Fi services to view the film at refugee centers in many cities in the Middle East and Europe. Micro secure digital (SD) cards—which don't require an internet connection to access the content—present short Christian films, sermons, and gospel presentations in the Arabic, Farsi, and Urdu languages and have been widely distributed in Greece, Germany, Sweden, and elsewhere.

Trans World Radio (TWR), a leading radio broadcast ministry, has develop an app called Refugee Bridge that features several of their audio programs specially prepared for refugees. Currently over 340 episodes in Arabic, Farsi, and Dari are offered; and new episodes are being added every week, keeping refugees constantly engaged. Several Iranian Christian ministries in London and Amsterdam have developed refugee-specific audio and video content over the last two years, and they have reported unexpected and remarkable receptivity and impact in sharing the gospel with Iranians seeking shelter in Europe.

Jesuit Refugee Services provides education to refugees in Kakuma in Kenya and Dzaleka in Malawi. Church World Services has given out basic-feature phones to Somali refugees in the US, helping them to use banking apps and to stay in touch with families and friends back home. Other organizations have used ESL classes and training apps on phones and tablets to help Burmese refugees acquire important language proficiency and better integrate into the Western world. Cloud-based translation tools have removed the barrier of interacting with someone who speaks a different language, helping both parties acquire new language skills while deepening their friendship across religious and cultural lines. Churches and ministries in Canada have mobilized old computers and phones from their members on behalf of newly arriving refugees in their community.

Many Christians have used technology and social media considerably for advocacy and for mobilizing resources for refugees arriving in their cities. The ways of leveraging technology in serving today's refugees are limitless, and we must use all the tools at our disposal to extend hospitality and to help them integrate well into our societies and nations.

CONCLUSION

Smartphones, combined with the internet and other technological tools have proven to be strategically critical tools in the hands of contemporary refugees, enabling the creation of unregulated safe-migration pathways that are fast and affordable for an increasing number of people who are forcibly displaced from the conflicts zones of the world. With ubiquitous connectivity and "appification," a wide range of tools running on handheld devices have become absolutely essential requirements for refugee movements. More churches and ministries working with refugees need to develop relevant content and tools to reach and serve refugees effectively. This will continue to be a highly impactful strategy to connect with and minister to people who are mobile, regardless of the cause or which part of the world they came from or are going to.

chapter eighteen

Becoming a Welcomer:
Practical Ways to Serve Refugees and Obey Scripture

TABITHA MCDUFFEE

The pages of this book on refugee diaspora are filled with amazing accounts of various refugee movements throughout the world and stories about the ways God is using this movement of people to beautifully expand the global church. You have read how different Christians have chosen to respond to the global refugee crisis, whether through advocacy, counseling, justice, social work, peacemaking, and solidarity. But armed with all this knowledge, you may still be left with the question "How can *I* make a difference?"

If you're wondering how you can put your knowledge of the global refugee crisis into action in your own home, church, or neighborhood, then this chapter is for you. I want to walk through some practical and measurable ways that you can become a welcomer of refugees in obedience to God's Word. First, I will address the importance of welcome by briefly outlining a theology of hospitality. Second, I will list several obstacles to being a welcomer, along with how we can overcome them by growing a practical, day-to-day lifestyle of hospitality. Finally, I will include a list of resources that may help you continue to grow as a welcomer, ranging from books and blogs to organizations and conferences. My hope is that you will find ways to take what you have learned in this book on refugee diaspora and put it into action right away.

THE MINISTRY OF WELCOME

What comes to your mind when you hear the word *hospitality*? Do you think of opening your home for a dinner party, or hosting a family gathering around the holidays? In the twenty-first century, hospitality has come to refer to welcoming friends and family into our home. In the Bible, however, hospitality means something very different. The Greek word translated "hospitality" in the New Testament is *philoxenia*, which literally means "love of strangers." You may notice that the word looks similar to *xenophobia*, which also comes from the Greek and can be translated "fear of strangers." Hospitality, in the biblical sense, is not simply entertaining our friends and family for dinner; instead it is loving and welcoming complete strangers, even those whom we are tempted to fear.

In the Sermon on the Mount, Jesus turns many traditional Jewish teachings on their head. Over and over he cites a Jewish teaching by saying, "You have heard it said . . . ," and then he challenges each command with "But I say . . ." One of the teachings he challenges has to do with hospitality. He says,

> "You have heard the law that says, 'Love your neighbor' and hate your enemy. But I say, love your enemies! Pray for those who persecute you! . . . If you love only those who love you, what reward is there for that? Even corrupt tax collectors do that much. If you are kind only to your friends, how are you different from anyone else? Even pagans do that?" (Matthew 5:43–44, 46–47 NLT)

It sounds like religious folks in Jesus' day also had mixed up ideas about hospitality. They thought they were only obligated to extend hospitality to their neighbors—in other words, people who were like them. But Jesus made it clear that the mark of a true disciple is someone who extends love and hospitality to strangers as well.

Welcoming refugees is just one application of practicing the kind of hospitality Jesus commanded. Refugees travel from different countries and cultures, speak different languages, and may eat different food or wear different clothes. Unfortunately, Christians have not always loved refugees well in obedience to Jesus' teaching on hospitality. The vast majority of immigrants to the US will never be invited into an American's home, let alone the home of an American who loves and follows Jesus. Refugees and immigrants who already love and follow Jesus rarely feel welcome in American churches, so they often establish churches specific to their ethnic or language group, which reflect their own unique music, worship style, timing, sermon delivery, illustrations, and social interactions within their church community. As a result, American and immigrant believers feel estranged from each other, even when they are living and worshiping in the same city or town.

For many Americans, their poor theology of hospitality is a result of a history of cultural superiority and ethnocentrism. Church leaders in dominant cultures often settle for the least common denominator of race and ethnicity, failing to adequately represent their changing neighborhoods or the increasing diversity within Christianity. But in recent decades the growing number of immigrant churches in the West has precipitated the growing de-Europeanization of American Christianity. Without a simultaneous emphasis on a theology of hospitality, this has only served to widen the chasm between Western and non-Western expressions of Christianity in the United States. Each of us normalizes our own cultural expression of the Christian faith and suspiciously views Christians who worship and practice their faith differently. These cultural differences, combined with power dynamics and economic issues, cloud our judgment when it comes to interacting with Christians who are unlike ourselves.

Most immigrants to the United States are Christians or embrace Christianity after encountering hospitable Christians in their neighborhoods, schools, or workplaces. Disobeying Christ's command to love and welcome strangers not only robs us of the opportunity to share the gospel with nonbelievers, but limits the maturity that Christians can gain through relationships with their fellow believers from other countries and cultures. I hope that over time the growing presence of Christian immigrants in our communities will help American Christians embrace their new social reality and rejoice in God's sovereignty over the movement of people around the world. This emerging context calls for genuine humility—a willingness to learn afresh about other cultures and people, to shed our parochial attitudes, and to develop a grander view of the global nature of Christianity and the missional opportunities that emerge as a result of global migration.

In *Welcoming the Stranger*, Patrick Keifert notes that hosting a stranger is usually a decentering experience and can recenter us from our individualistic and consumeristic worldviews.[1] When we approach the world of another with a willingness to learn and to be taught, we may realize that we are other to the others. By lending an ear, we indirectly give others a voice. By humbling ourselves and recognizing our own frailties, we can lift others up. By receiving from the stranger instead of always being the giver, we recognize that we are needy too. Receiving is much harder than giving because it keeps us from exerting and consolidating power on economic terms, so we often view newcomers, and particularly refugees, as people in need of material assistance; and we reduce

---

1 Patrick R. Keifert, *Welcoming the Stranger: A Public Theology of Worship and Evangelism* (Minneapolis: Fortress Press, 1992).

refugee ministries solely to providing handouts. In doing so, we fail to realize that by exposing our spiritual bankruptcy and self-reliant spirit, refugees give us far more than we give them. But it is exactly this role reversal that forces us come to terms with our shared humanity and begin to view others as people created in the image of God, regardless of the color of their skin, legal status, or economic means. As we enter into the world of another—identifying and interacting with them—our sense of being, notion of self, meaning in life, and ultimately our view of God and our mission in the world are transformed.

OBSTACLES TO BECOMING A WELCOMER

While many Christians may understand the scale of the global refugee crisis and the opportunity it presents to act in obedience to Jesus' teaching on hospitality, it can still be difficult to actually get started. We experience many obstacles to living out a life of true biblical hospitality, or we might even make excuses for not being a welcomer. Here are some common obstacles, along with how to overcome them, as we seek to obey Jesus' teaching to live hospitably in regard to refugees and others.

OBSTACLE 1: I'M TOO BUSY

Between our jobs, taking care of our families, and being involved in our churches, it can be difficult to find time to seek out and be hospitable to strangers. You may not be able to commit to formally volunteering with a refugee ministry, but there are countless ways to weave welcoming into the existing fabric of your life.

If your children attend a public school, it is quite possible that refugees and immigrants are your children's classmates. Consider reaching out to other parents at meetings, school activities, sports games, or drop-off or pick-up times. This is also an excellent opportunity to teach your children about the importance of loving and welcoming those who are different than them. Other ideas include visiting an ethnic restaurant or grocery store near your home or work, finding out where your taxi drivers are from, or striking up conversations with your neighbors. There are numerous ways to practice hospitality to strangers, even in the midst of your busyness.

OBSTACLE 2: I DON'T KNOW HOW TO TALK TO SOMEONE FROM ANOTHER CULTURE

Welcoming refugees and other immigrants can be intimidating. You might say the wrong thing and offend someone, or you might not know their language.

Any obedience to Jesus' command to love our neighbors is worth the risk of a potentially messy learning curve. Here are a few ways to make talking to someone from another culture go a bit more smoothly.

Show a genuine interest in the other person, and ask questions. Maintain a learning posture, and take notes on your conversation so that you can research more about their culture later. Develop a keen eye to locate people unlike you, and look up something about the people you meet or the state of Christianity in their part of the world. Read a good book on intercultural communication. But remember that no matter how much you read or how much training you receive, welcoming people from other cultures will inevitably involve some awkward situations—so sooner or later you just have to start that conversation!

OBSTACLE 3: HOSPITALITY IS NOT MY GIFT

Another obstacle to welcoming refugees is the belief that only certain kinds of people can be hospitable. This idea likely comes from our misunderstanding of hospitality as something that only happens when we invite large numbers of people into our homes. There are countless ways to practice hospitality, and every Christ-follower must find ways to be hospitable, no matter their personality type or gifting. If you are an introvert and not used to entertaining large groups of people, consider meeting refugees one-on-one to practice conversational English or volunteer to drive refugees who don't yet have a driver's license to their appointments. Rather than limiting us in our practice of hospitality, our individualities can help to inform our unique ministry of welcome and the ways we have been called to love the strangers God has placed in our path.

There are potentially many other obstacles to being a welcomer, but you must find ways to overcome them. Hospitality is not easy. Loving strangers takes intentionality and perseverance, but as we act in obedience to Jesus' teaching the blessings will far outweigh any inconveniences.

RESOURCES TO GROW AS A WELCOMER

Finally, I want to leave you with a list of resources that may be helpful to you as you continue to grow in the lifestyle of a welcomer, from books and blogs to organizations and conferences. First, don't set out on this journey of welcome alone. It works best in small groups of like-minded Christians who desire to grow as disciples of Christ by serving refugees and immigrants in their neighborhoods. Seeking support from others who have already been working with refugees will be invaluable and will help you avoid some common blunders. Many organizations are working in this space and actively involved in challenging and equipping Christians to do the hard work of hospitality. Christian organizations working to resettle refugees in the United States are Church World Service, Episcopal Migration Ministries, Lutheran Refugee Service, and World Relief.

The Refugee Highway Partnership, a global network of churches and organizations, equips Christians to welcome refugees (www.refugeehighway.net). World Vision is another international organization extensively involved with the global refugee crisis and helping to mobilize and deploy resources for refugees in many war zones and routes across the world (www.worldvision.org/our-work/ refugees). There are also countless Christian ministries working to support refugees during their first few months in the United States. You can find these by doing an internet search in your state or city. Several church denominations have also developed their own ministries for refugees and immigrants—for example, Catholic Relief Services, Catholic Charities, and Lutheran Immigration and Refugee Service.

In recent years, several new books have been written by Christians who are involved in hospitality and refugee ministries. I have found the following six books to be particularly helpful. The refugee advocates of World Relief together wrote *Seeking Refuge*,[2] which is an introduction to refugee issues from a Christian perspective. To understand the factors driving so many refugees and migrants to Europe in recent years, see *The New Odyssey*[3] which artfully blends investigative reporting with powerful storytelling. Two excellent books on biblical hospitality are *Making Room*, by Christine Pohl,[4] and *Christian Hospitality and Muslim Immigration in an Age of Fear*, by Matthew Kaemingk.[5] The former book shows how hospitality is central to Christian faith, while the latter addresses Islamophobia and anti-immigrant sentiments in the context of the Netherlands. *Assimilate or Go Home*[6] is a collection of essays written by a woman who has spent more than a decade living among refugees in Portland, Oregon. On a missiological perspective, *Strangers Next Door*[7] explains the incredible opportunities for mission arising out of global migration.

Several valuable and helpful free online resources are available for those interested in learning more. The United Nations High Commission for Refugees (www.unhcr.org) releases its Global Trends Report every year in

---

2   Stephan Bauman, Matthew Soerens, and Issam Smeir, *Seeking Refuge: On the Shores of the Global Refugee Crisis* (Chicago: Moody Press, 2016).

3   Patrick Kingsley, *The New Odyssey: The Story of the Twenty-First-Century* [per Amazon] Refugee Crisis (New York: Norton & Company, 2017).

4   Christine Pohl, *Making Room: Recovering Hospitality as a Christian Tradition* (Grand Rapids: Eerdmans, 1999).

5   Matthew Kaemingk, *Christian Hospitality and Muslim Immigration in an Age of Fear* (Grand Rapids: Eerdmans, 2018).

6   Danielle L. Mayfield, *Assimilate or Go Home: Notes from a Failed Missionary on Rediscovering Faith* (San Francisco: HarperOne, 2016).

7   J. D. Payne, *Strangers Next Door: Immigration, Migration and Mission* (Downers Grove, IL: InterVarsity, 2012).

June, which includes the latest statistics on refugee movements around the world. The Refugee Studies Centre at Oxford University (www.rsc.ox.ac.uk) has the latest academic research related to forced migration studies and international refugee law. Refugees Deeply (www.newsdeeply.com/refugees) is an independent digital media project dedicated to covering the global refugee crisis. Experts in the fields of journalism, policy, international development, humanitarian aid, advocacy, and more offer insights into the current events causing refugees to flee.

In 2014, I started FaithandForcedMigration.com, a blog and online resource, with the intent of encouraging those involved in welcoming ministries and challenging Christians to think about refugee movements from a biblical perspective. See also my recent ebook, *Refugees in the Bible*, which highlights the stories of six biblical refugees and the way their experiences are paralleled in the modern-day refugee crisis. In 2017, Jessica Udall, who has years of experience welcoming refugees and international students in the United States and overseas, launched LovingtheStrangerBlog.com. Her practical tips and resources for effective hospitality and her warm, joyful style of writing is so encouraging.

There are also conferences that focus on refugee ministries, such as the Refugee Roundtable organized by the Refugee Highway Partnership, which is the largest annual conference in North America and Europe for refugee practitioners from nonprofits and church ministries. Another helpful event is the Justice Conference, which focuses broadly on issues of biblical justice such as race, poverty, immigration, and the refugee crisis.

CONCLUSION

The true meaning of biblical hospitality is at the heart of welcoming strangers. The journey of weaving a love of strangers into the very tapestry of daily life will not happen overnight. Learning the art of biblical hospitality is a lifelong discipleship matter. It takes a great deal of intentionality, a growing awareness of changes in our immediate surroundings and in the world, and a continual development of intercultural skills. But most of all it requires a longing to reflect God's heart for the marginalized in our world as we navigate the difficult terrain of Christian hospitality in an inhospitable world.

SECTION C:

Reflections (Biblical, Theological, and Missiological)

chapter nineteen

A Shared Human Condition:
An Old Testament Refugee Perspective

CHRIS WRIGHT, PhD

In Old Testament times, God's people's ethics regarding refugees rested on the strong foundations of gratitude to God and the reflection of God's character as revealed in his actions. How applicable is this to us today? Is it legitimate to consider ancient Israel's laws and institutions and scriptural narratives and prophecies as providing any kind of authority in modern society? If we see that the Israelites were intended by God to be a "light to the nations," and if we adopt a "paradigmatic" approach to Old Testament hermeneutics, then the answer is yes. The God whom we meet in the Old Testament is the redeemer and covenant Lord of Israel, the giver and owner of their land and moral judge of all that happened there. If this is the same God who is the sovereign Lord of all nations, creator of the whole earth, and moral judge of all human history, then it is legitimate to make responsible connections between the ethical standards and motivations contained in the Old Testament and Christian reflection on social, economic, and political realities today.

Israel's conquest of Canaan might seem to contradict this, however. Are not the Old Testament's teachings on love toward foreigners negated by the violent treatment of the Canaanites? Briefly, the conquest was a unique and historically limited event, not a pattern for all future dealings with foreigners. It was explicitly justified on an ethical basis, namely as divine judgment on a society that had become morally degraded. Since the time of Abraham, the culture had deteriorated (Gen 15; Lev 18; Deut 9). God warned Israel that he would bring judgment and expulsion upon them, too, if they went the way of the Canaanites. The conquest was an integral part of the overarching biblical narrative of God's engagement with the fallen realities of the world, culminating in bringing salvation through the cross and resurrection of Christ.

A SHARED HUMAN CONDITION

Migration runs like a thread through the whole Bible narrative. People on the move are so much a part of the fabric of the story that we hardly notice it as a major feature. Indeed, when the text actually points out that Yahweh, the God of Israel, has been involved in the migrations of peoples other than Israel, some Bible translations put that affirmation in parentheses, as though to separate it off from the main story, even though it is an integral part of the entire theological context. Yahweh is the God of all nations and all their historical migrations and settlements (Deut 2:10–12,20–23). God's people began and continue their journey through history as "foreigners and strangers"—as migrants, immigrants, and occasionally refugees. This is part of our theological and historical DNA since Abraham. (Examples include Gen 23:4; Ex 2:22; Lev 25:23; Deut 23:7; 26:5; Ruth; Babylonian exile; etc.) Within the framework of God's sovereignty in human history and geography, migration, displacement, and mixing of nations are essential parts of the biblical narrative.

In recent years, millions of economic migrants and refugees have arrived in Europe. Such people movements have been part of human history for millennia, and God is not uninvolved or uninterested in them. As people who take the Bible seriously, we are called to try to see our contemporary movements in the light of God's story. In the midst of human crises of tragic proportions, we are invited to try to perceive the kingdom of God at work like yeast, or mustard seed, or a net, or any of the other metaphors that Jesus provided to help us understand. Migrations are part of God's ongoing story.

Because the Israelites themselves had been refugees and foreigners in Egypt, their law repeatedly emphasized caring for foreigners in their midst, especially those who were vulnerable and easy to exploit. Indeed, they were commanded to love the foreigner as much as they loved their neighbor and even themselves (Lev 19:18,34; Deut 10:19–20). Israel's story shaped Israel's ethic.

Most Western nations have experienced centuries of immigration. The US and Australia owe their current way of life almost entirely to immigration, some of it soaked in blood and oppression. In the UK, whole areas of the national economy could not function were it not for imported labor. Yet somehow political voices in these countries have become hostile to refugees and immigrants. They want to pull up the drawbridge and keep others out. There is blatant hypocrisy in this rhetoric. There is hypocrisy even in the language terms that are used. When Britishers, for example, go overseas in search of better economic opportunities, they are called "expatriates," while those who come to Britain seeking the same opportunity are vilified as "migrants."

There is also hypocrisy embedded in the lack of historical perspective. Some five hundred years ago Europeans decided to migrate worldwide. They exported themselves all over the globe: sometimes conquering, sometimes colonizing, often both. They asked no permission and needed no visas. They just went and took and stayed for centuries. Now the world bounces back. A tragic number of the crises in war-torn regions can be traced to the gross historical injustices of European expansionism, colonialism, the slave trade, and the scramble for Africa and the Middle East after the First World War. Simply stating this does not provide solutions to the dire problems of millions pouring into Europe from Islam's civil war in the Middle East. Still, it should nurture humility instead of false superiority as we consider the issues, and as we pray into them.

BIBLICAL DEFINITIONS

Before the Babylonian exile, Israel recognized different varieties of "foreigners," as reflected in terminology and legislation. As a state (and later two separate kingdoms), Israel was itself a mixed community. Strict Israelite ethnicity claimed descent from Abraham through the twelve tribes. However, Israel also included other groups. As early as the Exodus, they were a "mixed multitude," presumably because many groups of oppressed slaves joined them as they fled Egypt (Ex 12:37–39). As a result, the regulations for the Passover laid down what was permissible for such groups (Ex 12:43–49).

Palestine has always been a land bridge between competing powers. In biblical times it was the crossroads between Egypt, Mesopotamia (Iraq), and the Anatolian nations to the north (Turkey). Economic and military factors propelled constant migrations to and through the land that Israel came to possess. Thus Solomon's census recorded a substantial community of foreigners resident in his kingdom. He used 153,600 of them for manual labor of various sorts.

THREE WORDS FOR FOREIGNERS
IN THE OLD TESTAMENT ARE:

1. *Ezrah* is the term used (though not very often) for a native-born Israelite, resident by God's gift and grant within the land of Israel.

2. *Gēr* (plural gērîm), is the most common term. It is usually translated "alien" or "foreigner," but its social and economic meaning is more nuanced.[1] *Gērîm* were not ethnic Israelites, but were resident in the land, sometimes as members of Israelite households. They did not have a share in the land itself, but many would have been employed to work on the land. They were different than slaves, as they were free, and different than visiting foreigners (*nokrî'îm*), as they were more permanent residents. But their status was economically and socially weak and vulnerable since they lacked the security of land ownership and the strong ties of Israelite kinship in the tribal system.

We may understand the *gērîm* as persons from another tribe, city, district, or country who had left their homeland and who were no longer directly related to their original setting. They lacked the customary social protection of privilege and had, of necessity, placed themselves under the jurisdiction of someone else. Hence, it is sensible to suggest that the noun gér should be translated "immigrant." The phrase "resident alien" is awkward, and the term "sojourner" is archaic. "Immigrant" adds the motif of "social conflict." People became gérîm as a result of social and political upheaval such as war, famine, oppression, plague, and other social misfortunes. This term indicates the immigrant's "outsider" status in the adopted social setting.[2]

3. *Nokrîyîm* and *zārîm*. These were the true aliens or "strangers"—that is, foreigners who came from outside the land of Israel, had no natural link to the land, and were temporary visitors, perhaps as traveling merchants or mercenary soldiers. They were more independent outsiders, to whom some of the laws of life within the Israelite community did not apply. For example, they could be charged interest (Deut 23:20) and the sabbatical year cancellation of debt did not apply to them (Deut 15:3). They were less vulnerable than gērîm, and the text often speaks of them with a degree of suspicion or antagonism, primarily because they worshiped other gods and so posed a religious threat.

---

1 See Jonathan Burnside, *The Status and Welfare of Immigrants: The Place of the Foreigner in Biblical Law and Its Relevance to Contemporary Society* (Jubilee Centre, 2001), 10–16.

2 Ibid., 13–14.

Nevertheless, Solomon's prayer at the dedication of the temple expressed the surprising assumption that they could be attracted to come and worship the God of Israel in his temple so that Yahweh would answer their prayer, with amazing missional consequences for Yahweh's reputation worldwide (1 Kgs 8:41–43). Similarly, Isaiah 56:3–7 holds out the eschatological (and equally missional) promise that foreigners would come to be accepted in God's house, and their offerings at his altar (cf. Isa 60:10; 61:5–6). Such texts breathe the missional air of the Abrahamic covenant's promise in regard to all nations, that Abraham's descendants would be a blessing to all the families of the earth (Gen 12:3).

The *gērîm* were most like what we today call "immigrants" or "refugees" or "migrants." Accordingly, we will concentrate on that group in the following survey of legal and prophetic texts that show how Israel was expected to treat such people within their community.

ISRAEL'S LAW ON IMMIGRANTS/MIGRANTS/REFUGEES

Israel's law adopts a remarkably positive stance toward the *gērîm*. They are regularly listed alongside other categories of vulnerable people who need protective justice and social inclusion, such as widows, orphans, and the poor. Israel was to reflect in their own society the express concern of their God for the landless, the family-less, and the homeless. Far more than a sentimental generalization, this took specific legal shape, as the following texts indicate.

PROTECTION FROM GENERAL ABUSE AND OPPRESSION

"Do not mistreat or oppress a foreigner, for you were foreigners in Egypt" (Ex 22:21). "When a foreigner resides among you in your land, do not mistreat them" (Lev 19:33).

PROTECTION FROM UNFAIR TREATMENT IN COURT

"Do not oppress a foreigner; you yourselves know how it feels to be foreigners, because you were foreigners in Egypt" (Ex 23:9). "I charged your judges at that time, 'Hear the disputes between your people and judge fairly, whether the case is between two Israelites or between an Israelite and a foreigner residing among you. Do not show partiality in judging; hear both small and great alike'" (Deut 1:16–17). "Do not deprive the foreigner or the fatherless of justice, or take the cloak of the widow as a pledge. Remember that you were slaves in Egypt and the Lord your God redeemed you from there. That is why I command you to do this" (Deut 24:17–18).

INCLUSION IN SABBATH REST

Sabbath rest was a key innovation in Israelite economic and social culture. "Observe the Sabbath day by keeping it holy, as the Lord your God has commanded you. Six days you shall labor and do all your work, but the seventh day is a Sabbath to the Lord your God. On it you shall not do any work, neither you, nor your son or daughter, nor your male or female servant, nor your ox, your donkey or any of your animals, nor any foreigner residing in your towns, so that your male and female servants may rest, as you do" (Deut 5:12–14; cf. Ex 20:8–11).

INCLUSION IN WORSHIP AND COVENANT

Gērîm were to be included in the whole life of the community, provided they were assimilated through the rite of circumcision. For example, they could partake of the Passover, if circumcised (Ex 12:45–49). They benefited from the triennial tithe, a social fund for the destitute (Deut 14:28–29; 26:12–13). They were included in the joy and holiday of the annual feasts (Deut 16). They must observe the Day of Atonement (Lev 16:29). They were to be present at occasions of covenant renewal and the reading of the law (Deut 29:10–13; 31:12).

FAIR EMPLOYMENT PRACTICE

In the slave laws of Exodus and Deuteronomy, "Hebrews" probably were not ethnic Israelites but a social class of people, similar in some ways to *gērîm*, who lived by selling their labor—a kind of "underclass," possibly related to the *'apîru*, a socially rootless class of people known across the ancient Near East. This category of people, something like migrant workers, were to be given their freedom after six years of service—i.e., effectively a six-year contract—after which the "Hebrew" was free either to leave or to make his relationship with that household permanent at his own choice, not his master's pleasure (Ex 21:1–11; Deut 15:12–18).

PROMPT PAYMENT OF WAGES

This was another concern of Israel's employment law. In this case, the *gērîm* are listed alongside "hired workers." Such people, often working for daily wages, were (and still are) an easy target for exploitation and ill-treatment. Neglect of paying a fair day's wage for a fair day's work is counted not just as carelessness but as "guilty of sin." "Do not take advantage of a hired worker who is poor and needy, whether that worker is a fellow Israelite or a foreigner residing in one of your towns. Pay them their wages each day before sunset, because they are poor and are counting on it. Otherwise they may cry to the Lord against you, and you will be guilty of sin" (Deut 24:14–15).

ACCESS TO AGRICULTURAL PRODUCE—GLEANING RIGHTS

Since *gērîm* did not have a share in the distribution of the land, they were dependent on the Israelite households for whom they worked to be able to enjoy the fruitfulness of the land. And God insisted that since the land was his anyway (as the supreme landlord—Lev 25:23), then the landless must be given the opportunity to feed themselves, to "eat and be satisfied" (Ps 22:26) along with the rest of the population (Lev 19:9–10; Deut 24:19–22).

RIGHT OF ASYLUM AND NONRETURN

Slaves who run away from their masters have universally been subject to severe punishment across all human cultures that have had slavery as part of their society. And those who harbor runaway slaves likewise expose themselves to legal penalties. That was so in the cultures surrounding ancient Israel—which makes Israel's law on the matter so surprising, since it was the diametric opposite. "If a slave has taken refuge with you, do not hand them over to their master. Let them live among you wherever they like and in whatever town they choose. Do not oppress them" (Deut 23:15–16).

Now, granted, this is a law concerning slaves, not strictly immigrants or refugees. Nevertheless, one assumes that the reason a slave would seek refuge is that he or she was suffering cruelty or some other form of injustice and oppression. The principle of the law surely therefore applies to those in a comparable situation today who are fleeing from unbearable circumstances. There is a difference between the few refugees that this law seems to assume[3] and the mass exodus of millions of refugees that we see in today's world. But the assumption of the law is surely that people have a right to escape ill-treatment and to choose an alternative place to live.

---

3 If large numbers ran away, slavery would soon cease to exist; the law therefore is evidence that slavery in ancient Israel did not reflect the horrendous inhumanity that we associate with Roman galley slaves and black African slaves in the Americas.

EQUALITY BEFORE THE LAW WITH NATIVE-BORN

This is possibly the most radical and far-reaching of all Israel's laws relating to foreigners. While there were clear religious, social, and economic distinctions between ethnic Israelites and non-Israelite *gērîm* regarding the Israelites' sustaining covenantal network of kinship and land, nevertheless the foreigners were to be treated with equality in any legal dispute or criminal proceedings. Indeed, the same love commandment that applied to "your neighbor" (a fellow Israelite) was to be obeyed in relation to the foreigner: "Love them as yourself" (Lev 19:34; note the balance with v. 18).

Taken all together, this is a remarkable list of laws and exhortations relating to the treatment of foreigners and immigrants. The strongest word that is used to summarize it all is the love command. The expression "You shall love . . . " (the second-person singular waw-consecutive qal perfect of *'āhab*) occurs only four times in the Old Testament. Two express what Jesus called the first and second greatest commandments in the law: love for God and love for neighbor (Deut 6:4–5; Lev 19:18). The other two command God's people to love the immigrant: "For the Lord your God is God of gods and Lord of lords, the great God, mighty and awesome, who shows no partiality and accepts no bribes. He defends the cause of the fatherless and the widow, and loves the foreigner residing among you, giving them food and clothing. And you are to love those who are foreigners, for you yourselves were foreigners in Egypt" (Deut 10:17–19; also Lev 19:34).

The motivation for such laws is threefold. The first is Israel's own history. Those who had experienced what it was like to be an exploited ethnic immigrant community—originally famine refugees—must show compassion to others in similar circumstances. The second motivation is the character of Yahweh, the God of Israel, revealed in his historic actions. Those who worship him must walk in his ways and live by his values and priorities. The third motivation is the desire for God to continue to bless his people. This will happen if they respond to his prior grace and redemptive blessing by showing comparable compassion and justice to the poor in their own midst.

In other words, Israel's ethic in relation to refugees was built on the strong foundations of gratitude to God for what he had done and the reflection of the character of God as revealed in those actions. Stated negatively, among the list of curses for covenant disobedience is this: "'Cursed is anyone who withholds justice from the foreigner, the fatherless or the widow.' Then all the people shall say, 'Amen!'" (Deut 27:19).

When we read the narratives of Israel's history in the land as seen through the eyes of the prophets, God's key complaints are often against injustice and oppression of the poor. Sometimes this focuses specifically on treatment of foreigners and immigrants.

For example, though Moab was an inveterate enemy of the two Israelite kingdoms, and though several prophets include Moab in their oracles expressing God's judgment on surrounding nations, nevertheless Isaiah called upon the political leaders of Judah to respond to the plight of Moab's refugees during a military crisis that had caused their population (including vulnerable women) to flee (Isa 16:2–5). In another situation, Jeremiah condemned the people of Judah for failing to care for the needy among them while they carried on with obsessive worship in the temple. This was one of the social sins for which God eventually would expel them from the land and the temple (Jer 7:6–7).

The same prophet told the government that unless they changed their policy toward such needy people they would lose the legitimacy and authority of their office altogether. Notably, ill-treatment of foreigners/immigrants is placed in the same moral category as shedding innocent blood (Jer 22:3). Ezekiel has the same scale of ethical values, accusing the political leadership of Judah of exactly these things, setting them alongside other violations of Israel's worship and covenant commitments (Ezek 22:6–9, 29).

Right to the very end of the Old Testament, this remains a matter of pressing concern for God, according to the prophets. The "day of the Lord" will bring judgment on his people, and one of the primary reasons is their treatment of the needy, including immigrants (Mal 3:5). The quantity of biblical material on this theme is massive. The scale of statute laws, ethical exhortations, historical and theological motivations, and prophetic condemnations around this issue surely marks it as a major concern of biblical faith and life. God really cares about the treatment of outsiders, migrants, refugees, immigrants.

By comparison, the Old Testament has some very clear teaching about God's standards for sexual behavior. These teachings permeate the law, the narratives, the prophets, and the wisdom literature. The Bible clearly condemns deviations from God's sexual standards. Yet these condemnations are outweighed in volume by the deluge of texts dealing with God's concern for justice and compassion for marginalized people, including the persistent mention of foreigners and immigrants. Among Christians who claim to honor, believe, and obey the Bible, how does this weigh in the scale of our moral values? Do we share anywhere near the same degree of ethical concern, let alone political passion, for refugee immigrants?

CONCLUSION

This Old Testament prescription for life has both ethical and missional implications. First, it describes the nature of humanity and the basis for human rights as rooted in the truth that all people are created in the image of God. All have dignity. All are equal (Job 31:13–15; Prov 14:31; 17:5; 22:2). Such human rights are the obverse of responsibilities, biblically speaking. Those responsibilities are both vertical and horizontal. Worship of the God who is transcendent demands respect and care for our fellow human beings.

A second implication addresses the nature of ethnicity, the state, and our political duty. Ethnic and cultural diversity result from God's gift of creativity. They are part of God's creation (Deut 32:8; Acts 17:26) and will be preserved in the new creation (Rev 7:9). Therefore, protecting cultural heritages and identities is worthwhile. Regarding the state and government, the church has a prophetic role. The primary duty of government is to judge righteously and defend the right of the poor and marginalized (Ps 72:4,12–14; Prov 31:1–9, Jer 22:1–4; Rom 13:1–4); and the primary duty of God's people, beyond loving God, is to "Love your neighbor as yourself" (Lev 19:18) and "Love the alien as yourself" (Lev 19:34 NRSV).

A third implication relates to gospel and mission. In its essence, the gospel breaks down barriers of race and cultural prejudice (Eph 2:11–3:6). The Old Testament prophets envisioned the nations being gathered to Israel and blessed through the line of Abraham (Isa 19:19–25; 56:3–8; 60:3; Zech 2:11; etc.). Such centripetal gathering complements centrifugal missions. Today, through the flood of refugees, the nations are gathering in our lands and our communities. This opens new opportunities for missions (Jer 29:1–14, especially v. 7). We must place current global migration and refugee issues within the framework of God's sovereignty to see the opportunities in the light of God's mission, and to see the future in the light of God's ultimate promise.

chapter twenty

Relationship and Scripture in Practical Refugee Ministry

PAUL N. SYDNOR

Nine months earlier, Marjan had applied for asylum in France and received the documents required for the process. Subsequently, she submitted the papers to the officials, but they weren't returned to Marjan like they should have been. Without these papers Marjan couldn't carry on with the asylum process, so she asked her friend Elizabeth from church to go with her to ask about the documents.

Through the heavy glass window, Elizabeth explained that Marjan needed the documents to continue the asylum process for her protection as a Christian. But doubting Marjan's claim to be a Christian, the official turned to her and demanded, "When is Easter?"

Expecting to hear a date, the official looked bewildered when Marjan replied, "Easter is when Jesus died on the cross and then rose again to return to heaven."

Turning then to Elizabeth and speaking in a heavy dialect, the official asked, "Why is she worried about her documents? She will be deported anyhow!"

Knowing that Marjan understood some of the dialect and seeing the tears in her eyes, Elizabeth protested that this was for the judge to decide and demanded that the official, as a public servant, carry out his job properly and return Marjan's official documents.

The Refugee Highway Partnership (RHP) considered exchanges like this in its "Best Practices for Christian Ministry among Forcibly Displaced People."[1] This document was drafted at the global consultation of the RHP that was convened by the World Evangelical Alliance in 2001 in Izmir, Turkey. The "Best Practices" include twenty-one principles divided into seven sections about ministry policy and practice; the role of advocacy, the role of the church, the role of refugees, the role of organizations, ministry context, and partnership. This chapter highlights various principles of the "Best Practices" to illustrate that at its core refugee ministry is relational, connects refugees to Scripture, and is practical.

THE RELATIONAL DIMENSION OF REFUGEE MINISTRY

The first aspect of Christian ministry among refugees is relationship. Christian refugee work is not primarily about meeting needs or even leading others to Christ; it is more than merely a project to be managed. Refugee ministry workers are relational mediators who model their ministry after God's own relationship in the Trinity and in the example of Jesus, who came to reconcile humanity with God.

Principle #1 of the "Best Practices" states, "Effective refugee ministry has relationship with God and people at its core." The indicators of this characteristic include:

- Service is motivated by love for God and love for people.

- Prayer is an integral part.

- Refugees are encouraged to seek and call upon God.

- Refugees have opportunities to hear the story of Jesus.

- Reconciliation with both God and humanity are promoted among all people.

Like these indicators suggest, relational ministry takes a person-to-person approach that puts the ministry on a grassroots level of common humanity. This kind of ministry develops relationships that break the dehumanizing cycle of displacement, along with the rejection and trauma that refugees experience. Through relationship, people realize that another human being cares about them and what they say and do.

When a community of persecuted Christians relocated to Europe, their leader tried to connect with local church leaders. A mutual friend helped the leaders

---

1 Available at http://www.refugeehighway.net/uploads/5/4/1/8/54189183/refugee_ministry_best_prac-tices_2016.pdf (accessed March 1, 2018).

meet together; and finally, after three years, the various leaders began to see the part they could play in the other's community. Reflecting on this relationship, the friend said, "Often I only repeated the same thing that each would say to the other. I was simply a bridge between them."

Giving food or medicine, providing shelter and even language instruction, are important services, but relationship makes a person more than a passive recipient—but rather a fellow stakeholder in a mutual experience. Whether carried out by a local church, an international organization, or by refugees themselves, a relational emphasis underlines the dignity and value of the human context.

The concern for context in the "Best Practices" considers the regional, cultural, political, and historical background (Principle 18); it makes the ministry flexible and responsive to changing conditions (Principle 19); and it informs all ministry activity (Principle 20). In a relational ministry, the concern for context hears the plea of refugees who say, "We just want to be treated as human beings." If refugee ministry does not regard the human context of displacement, then it could face the dilemma that Dietrich Bonhoeffer described as "so little ground under their feet."[2] Without the ground of humanity, refugee ministry will lose its credibility.

A relational ministry stands on human ground before it touches holy ground. The human factor, like topography on a map, makes ministry three-dimensional. Building relationship with refugees is like shining a light into a dark room to see the situation in the room as it really is, not just as it has been imagined or stumbled over in the dark. The example at the asylum office involves the national context of the official as well as Marjan's personal context as a foreigner. The relationship between Elizabeth and Marjan, however, reflects a mutual human experience that says, "Before I am a citizen of any country, rich or poor, a Christian or not, I am a human being made in the image of God." It puts each person into the same boat to receive and understand life as given by the Creator.

THE SCRIPTURAL CONNECTION OF REFUGEE MINISTRY

In addition to being relational, Christian ministry among refugees makes a connection to Scripture. Scripture is the basis for understanding God's reality, and this awareness builds through interaction and relationship with others.

---

2 Dietrich Bonhoeffer, "After Ten Years," in *Letters and Papers from Prison*, vol. 8 of Dietrich Bonhoeffer Works, 1st English ed. (Minneapolis: Fortress, 2010), 19–41. In his evaluation of the German National Socialist Party in 1939, Bonhoeffer addressed what it means to live as Christians in an evil age. He identified six fallacies in the treatment of other human beings that undercut the essential value of being created in the image of God. He referenced the Israelites in 2 Chronicles as an example of people under the threat of displacement.

When one refugee was suddenly and unjustly held in detention, he said, "I had never even seen a prison, and I struggled with the trauma of this." He had not expected this kind of treatment. Yet, other refugees in the prison understood his trauma and invited him to read the Scriptures. Together they discussed the story of Joseph in Genesis 19. He realized, "If God was with Joseph in prison, he could also be with me." His relationship to the other refugees, and their unofficial church in the prison, served as his advocate to help him see his experience in the light of God's Word.

The connection to Scripture advocates for God's reality. The "Best Practices" includes principles for advocacy. Principle 8 notes that advocacy is "grace-based, honest and performed with integrity." It is most effective when done "in collaboration with refugees" (Principle 9) and when "the local church plays a vital role" (Principle 10). Advocacy in refugee ministry addresses the reality and concerns of both Scripture and refugees.

The reality for most refugees is that the trauma and injustice of displacement will likely not cease when they find resettlement. Refugees will face unmet expectations and broken dreams, and even after they flee they will still experience violence, conflict, and discrimination. Indeed, many refugees are like Job, who struggled to understand and accept the reality of his circumstances. Job longed for the "months of old" when he was "washed with butter," "sat as a chief," and "lived like a king" (Job 29 ESV). By the end of Job's story, he had wrestled in his prayers, shared with his friends, and pleaded for justice and vindication (Job 31). Only after these exchanges and coming to terms with his own situation, could Job accept God's reality (Job 38–41). Job's response to the Lord relates to refugees today: "I know that you can do all things, and that no purpose of yours can be thwarted. . . . I had heard of you by the hearing of the ear, but now my eye sees you" (Job 42:2,5 ESV).

Effective ministry relates refugee realities to God's reality through prayers, conversation, and sharing with others. This kind of ministry knows that the way to finding more hope in a broken and desperate situation is to see more of God's reality. It addresses the humanitarian concerns of refugees equally alongside the questions of faith. Many churches are ineffective and paralyzed in their understanding of refugee ministry because they address the humanitarian and faith issues as two separate concerns. They believe the government or large NGOs will take care of refugees' humanitarian needs, while the church responds only to those who show spiritual interest. The concern to give equal treatment and not to manipulate others is important. However, to separate the spiritual from the human relegates the gospel to one corner of understanding. This reflects an incomplete view of God's activity in the world.

God puts his image into every human being, and there is no experience that exists apart from the image of God. When ministry connects to Scripture, it resembles the life of Christ. It connects to the image of God, which—like Christ, as the perfect image of God—holds the human and spiritual reality in balance. God builds his kingdom by pouring into the experience of a refugee and charting a new course for the person. To understand the direction that God takes is like navigating a map and requires interaction with others along the way. To connect refugees with Scripture is not the same as reaching a people group. The kingdom of God is larger than a single national perspective and in Christ there is reconciliation beyond the failed states and broken people of world.

Christian refugee ministry helps displaced people hear God, reflect on their connection to God, and see their reality honestly. For one refugee, the knowledge that God's perspective is larger than the suffering and death he had experienced helped him to be strong. Reflecting on the events of his journey, and the loss of family and friends, he noted, "Anyone who says there is no God is dead already." While such experiences cause some to doubt God, for him—like Job—his connection to God was his source of humility, hope, and salvation.

When refugees make the connection between themselves and Scripture, they turn toward a perspective beyond the limits of displacement. As one man expressed it, "I can now see a light at the end of the tunnel." Or as another said, "Until I saw Jesus, faith and hope were untouchable, like honey on the inside of a jar."

To connect refugees with Scripture is to follow Jesus in the many episodes of his own journey toward the Cross.[3] The good news in refugee ministry is more than a decision to follow Christ or a prayer to defy the consequences of sin. Rather, it includes the life-giving perspective of God as a good shepherd who sees, hears, and cares for those who walk the paths of Christ himself in his journey to the Cross.

THE PRACTICAL ASPECTS OF REFUGEE MINISTRY

Finally, the crown of refugee ministry is its practical nature. Principle 7 says that refugee ministry (specifically advocacy) should benefit refugees; it should actually accomplish something on their behalf. Ministry is practical when the relationships that develop pursue realistic results and the connection to Scripture is applied to life. Many of the indicators of best practices are practical

---

3 See Luke 9:51–19:44.

in nature.[4] Principles 4 and 6 stress the need for assessment and learning, while principles 9 and 11 emphasize the need for collaboration and the use of external resources to increase effectiveness. Finally, principles 12 and 13 highlight the importance of direct refugee involvement in shaping the vision and mission of the work.

The continuum drafted by International Association for Refugees (IAFR) provides a helpful illustration of practical ministry.[5]Refugees are forced to flee for various reasons, and this leads to the loss of basic needs for survival. Although life is stabilized when these needs are restored, the victims have not fully recovered. This illustrates emergency needs on the one hand, as well as the various areas of recovery and the rebuilding of normal life on the other. No matter where refugee ministry engages along the continuum, there is a practical outcome.

Elizabeth's accompanying Marjan to the asylum office was a practical step that resulted in securing Marjan's documents. Practical activities also include hospitality. We often invite refugees to our house for a meal, and in one recent conversation around the table we discussed what hope means. A Congolese asylum-seeker said, "Sitting here with you around this table is hope." Food and hospitality is an international language that refugees especially understand, and it establishes a network of new relationships which serve all parties well.

Prayer is another example of practical ministry. In 2017, twenty-five internally displaced women in Kenya prayed for God to expand their chicken-egg business. This would increase their contribution to the community and their capacity to provide for their families. Their prayers were answered through the partnership of IAFR and NCCK (National Council of Churches Kenya), which helped them purchase and build chicken coops for a thousand more chickens.[6]The practical nature of refugee ministry brings the relational and scriptural aspects of ministry together.

At the height of the refugee crisis in Europe in 2015, one church in northern France opened its doors to a group of unaccompanied minors who were sleeping in a nearby park. The minors found shelter in the church every night for over a year. Feeling overwhelmed and no longer able to continue this ministry, the small church invited the local community to join in finding a practical solution. In the

---

4 See Sadiri Joy Tira and Tetsunao Yamamori, *Scattered and Gathered: A Global Compendium of Diaspora Missiology* (Oxford: Regnum Books, 2016), which includes a section of specialized case studies, many of which are examples of best practices in refugee ministry.

5 "The Unique Role of IAFR on the Refugee Highway," International Association for Refugees, 2017, http://iafr.org/downloads/IAFRs Unique Role on the Refugee Highway -US Letter.pdf (accessed March 1, 2018).

6 "Mission Accomplished!" *The IAFR Blog*, December 15, 2017, http://iafr.org/blog/105-mission-accomplished-poultry-project-completed (accessed March 1, 2018).

next twelve months, the church helped find "foster homes" for over ninety refugee minors who were stranded on the streets.

Local churches like this make a practical impact as they find the avenues required for solutions. Church members like Elizabeth can connect with refugees and advocate on their behalf not only because they are local citizens and want to help, but also because they have the relational and spiritual DNA that is described in the Scriptures. They address the real needs of real people in desperate conditions in the context of forceful displacement by becoming agents of love, mercy, justice, and reconciliation in a broken world.

CONCLUSION

The aspects of relationship and Scripture make refugee ministry balanced and holistic. These aspects see redeemed life as a reconciled connection between others and with God. No part of life is left untouched—whether social, political, cultural, or spiritual. All of these are joined in a realistic view of life. Through relationship, refugee ministry helps to make sense of displacement. It provides a human context for understanding the reality of displacement and the fullness of life described in the Scriptures. It puts into practice a kingdom view of mission rooted in God's image for humanity and God's sovereignty over human dispersion.

chapter twenty-one

Refugee Opportunity:
A Missional Responsibility of the Church

YOUSEF K ALKHOURI

"Your God hears prayer!" was a statement that I repeatedly heard from Syrian and Iraqi refugees during my visits to refugee camps in the Middle East. I heard numerous miracles of physical healing and personal encounters with the risen King. While many missionaries go to bring comfort to the refugees, they are often surprised to hear of the work of God's Spirit bringing hope, restoration, and redemption to them. The twenty-first century has been called the century of migration[1] and refugees, as a facet of migration has been a major concern globally, especially in light of the Syrian-Iraqi crisis. In this chapter I present some biblical reflections on the crisis of refugees and consider the role of the church as God's agent for mission in the context of the Syrian and Iraqi refugee crisis.

BIBLICAL REFLECTION

The Bible begins with a story of displacement from Eden. Rupen Das rightly explains that "displacement has always been a reality since the beginning of time."[2] Adam and Eve were expelled from the garden of Eden and began their journey of migration after the Fall. The Israelites, who are descendants of

---

1 Patrick Mwania Musau, "'I Was a Stranger and You Welcomed Me': A Christian Pastoral Response to Migration and Displacement," *African Ecclesiastical Review* 59, no. 1–2 (March 2017): 4–25.

2 Rupen Das, "Refugees: Exploring Theological and Missiological Foundations," *Journal Of European Baptist Studies* 16, no. 2 (January 2016): 33–47.

Abraham, himself a migrant from Ur, were once sojourners and constituted a displaced diaspora community in Egypt (Gen 17:8; Ex 22:21).[3]

The Hebrew Bible is rich with examples of prominent figures who experienced displacement. For example, Moses fled for his life to Midian after murdering an Egyptian (Ex 2:15) and he could be considered as a refugee.[4] David fled on numerous occasions, first from Saul and later from his son Absalom (1 Sam 21:10; 2 Sam 15:14–16). Naomi, Ruth, Elijah, Daniel, and numerous other characters in the Old Testament were refugees in a foreign land. The exiles to Assyria and Babylon were major displacements for the kingdoms of Israel and Judah (2 Kgs 17:23; 25:8–11; Esth 2:5–7; Ezek 17:11–14).

Displacement is a significant theme also in the New Testament. Matthew records the story of the holy family and Jesus fleeing from the brutality of Herod to Egypt (Matt 2:13–15). The incarnated God, Jesus Christ, was a Middle Eastern refugee. The African theologian Clement Majawa considers Jesus a "proto-refugee."[5] He lived as a refugee since he did not have a place to lay his head (Luke 9:58). Even in his death, Jesus was buried in a grave that was not his own (Matt 27:57–61).

The early church also endured the suffering of displacement. The author of Acts records that persecution became the catalyst to scatter the church throughout Judea and Samaria (Acts 8:1) and later to Phoenicia, Cyprus, and Antioch (Acts 11:19). The writer of the epistle to the Hebrews affirms that Abraham, as well as the church, lived as migrants and were looking for a heavenly city (Heb 11:10,16).

The Scriptures are replete with instructions on how to treat migrants who come for refuge to the people of God. In the book of Exodus, God commands the Israelites not to mistreat the foreigners among them, reminding them that they were also once foreigners (Lev 19:33–34). The Deuteronomic Code presents explicit commands on how the Israelites should treat the strangers in their land (Deut 24:20). Subsequently, failure to keep these commandments resulted in God's judgment of the Israelites (Isa 30:12–13). Those who forsake helping and protecting vulnerable and displaced people receive the strongest condemnation in the New Testament (Matt 25:35–40).

The theme of displacement and the people of God as migrants and refugees plays an important and central role throughout Scripture. Humanity is displaced from the garden of Eden as a result of the disobedience of Adam and Eve,

---

3 Musau, "'I Was a Stranger,'" 4–25

4 Craig Keener, "Moses as a Refugee—Exodus 2:15–17," *Bible Background*, last modified 2017, http://www.craigkeener.com/moses-as-a-refugee-exodus-215-17/ (accessed Jun 15, 2018).

5 Clement Majawa, "The African Refugee-Shepherding Ecclesiology," in *A Theological Response to the Tragedy of Refugees and Internally Displaced Persons in Africa*, ed. Sewe-K'Ahenda, 46; quoted in Musau, "'I Was a Stranger,'" 4–25.

and we as migrants are waiting for the heavenly Jerusalem (Heb 11:10; 13:14). It is crucial to notice that displacement proceeds to redemption and salvation. Catholic theologian Patrick M. Musau of Kenya contends, "The scripture puts migrants and displaced people at the centre of its salvation narrative."[6]

Hence it is impossible to read these narratives in the Bible without observing God's redemptive hand that appears vividly in the history of the people who suffer displacement, such as the Israelites in Egypt and later in exile. The Bible is a series of migratory narratives, as well as God's mission to redeem his creation. After the Fall, God promises salvation (Gen 3:16). He redeems the Israelites from slavery in Egypt, and he returns them to their homeland from the exile. He redeems the world through the offering of his Son (Eph 1:7; 1 Cor 1:30; Heb 9:12–14). And in the consummation, he restores his people from their displacement to an eternal home, the New Jerusalem.

MISSIONAL RESPONSIBILITY
AND OPPORTUNITY FOR THE CHURCH

God is as concerned for the Syrian and Iraqi refugees today as he was concerned for the Israelites and the early church. He is on a mission to redeem their sufferings and breathe new life into the body of Christ through them. The church is called to participate in God's mission. "The mission of the church flows from the mission of God and the fulfillment of God's mandate."[7] Therefore the church's mission to refugees is a responsibility, and presents a great and unprecedented opportunity.

The Great Commission for the church is to make new disciples of Jesus from all nations (Matt 28:19). Mission is the reason why the church exists. Therefore the church and its responsibility of mission are inseparable. Church and mission are so deeply intertwined that "We cannot biblically speak of mission apart from speaking of the church, and we cannot speak of the church apart from speaking also of mission."[8] The church is responsible for representing God's love and care for Middle Eastern refugees. It is a command and an obligation (Lev 19:33–34; Jer 22:3; Matt 22:39), not an option. God is working through the church, the community of God's people, to bring about his redemptive work among refugees.

---

6 Musau, "'I Was a Stranger,'" 4–25.

7 Christopher J. H. Wright, *The Mission of God: Unlocking the Bible's Grand Narrative*, Downers Grove: IVP Academic, 2006, 67.

8 Craig Ott, Stephen J. Strauss, and Timothy C. Tennent, *Encountering Theology of Mission: Biblical Foundations, Historical Developments, and Contemporary Issues* (Grand Rapids: Baker Academic, 2010), 193.

Many Western Christians remain ignorant, suspicious, and fearful of engaging with refugees because of radical Islamic terrorism. They fail to realize that Christianity began in the Middle East and the European garb of Christianity is a more recent happening. The Telegraph reported in January of 2017 about Muslim refugees coming to faith in Christ in Lebanon by attending a Bible study at an Anglican church. A fifty-seven-year-old Syrian refugee recalled, "Almost everyone attending the classes was Muslim. Mostly Syrian and Iraqi refugees. I'd never seen anything like it—Muslims singing about Jesus."[9] There are numerous accounts of churches in Europe and the Middle East where Muslim refugees are turning to Christ.[10] The church must recognize its divine calling to stand with and reach out to all marginalized people, including refugees, because they are created in the image of God and in need of God's redemption.

Christianity has been on the decline in the Middle East for the last fourteen hundred years since the rise of Islam. Syria and Iraq are among the most influential Muslim countries in the Middle East historically, and the majority of the populations in these countries are Muslims. According to the Joshua Project, 95 percent of Iraq's population are Muslims, of which over 72 percent are unreached. Similarly, Muslims account for 90 percent of the overall population in Syria, and 50 percent are unreached. After the recent wars in the region, many Muslims and non-Muslims have fled to neighboring countries and Europe. These unreached people have come closer to the gospel due to the refugee crisis.

Sam George is accurate in his recent assessment that "only God could have turned such a desperate situation into such a mission opportunity."[11] The forced migratory survival struggles present new opportunities for Christian witness in unexpected ways. This is an open door for mission and witness to Muslims from the Middle East, the likes of which we have not ever seen.

There are many ways in which the church can engage with Muslim refugees. There have always been hopes for opportunities to reach out and engage with Muslims, and a ministry to Middle Eastern refugees provides the church with numerous opportunities. Foremost, the church has a fundamental role to play in advocating for justice and confronting the oppression of Muslim migrants,

9 Josie Ensor, "The Muslim Refugees Converting to Christianity 'To Find Safety,'" The Telegraph, January 30, 2017, http://www.telegraph.co.uk/news/2017/01/30/muslim-refugees-converting-christianity-find-safety/ (accessed December 15, 2017).

10 To read more, see "Muslim Refugees Are Converting to Christianity in Germany," The Independent, December 9, 2016, http://www.independent.co.uk/news/world/europe/muslim-refugees-converting-to-christianity-in-germany-crisis-asylum-seekers-migrants-iran-a7466611.html (accessed December 15, 2017).

11 Sam George, "Is God Reviving Europe through Refugees?" Lausanne Global Analysis 6, no. 3 (May 2017), https://www.lausanne.org/content/lga/2017-05/god-reviving-europe-refugees (accessed January 5, 2018).

a vulnerable and marginalized group of people who have experienced forced displacement. The church has the potential to impact public opinion through teaching Christians about God's concern for migrants and mobilizing them for refugee ministry. Christians must learn to advocate for displaced people in the public arena and in democratic societies. The church has to leverage its social, political, and financial capital on behalf of refugees for the benefit of the mission of God among them.

Second, understanding the dynamics of migration and displacement reveals that people are open to new ideas and even consider a religious change in the process of migration. As Samuel Escobar observes, "Migrants—*including refugees*—are people in transition, experiencing the loss of roots and open to *new commitments*, ready to assume faith in a personal way."[12] Many Middle Eastern Muslims suffered the brutality of radical Islam in their countries. They fled for hope, security, and new pathways to worship God. Therefore people are more likely to find hope in the good news during their first stages of displacement. A newsletter on refugees in Germany states, "Thousands of refugees in Germany are converting from Islam to Christianity."[13]

In 2014, I had the chance to visit several refugees in countries that received large numbers of people affected by the civil war in Syria. I heard stories of escaping conflict zones and walking across deserts and borders. Some had been living in refugee camps for up to two years. They had received support and humanitarian aid from various international agencies, as well as Muslim and Christian relief workers. These refugees experienced God's love and redemption through his church, as believers offered them humanitarian support for their physical, emotional, and spiritual needs. Many refugees shared about miracles that happened when missionaries and Christian volunteers prayed for them in the name of Isa. Many had dreams and visions of Jesus or experienced God's supernatural intervention while fleeing from war zones. The kindness and prayers of missionaries and the miracles had turned them toward the living God in new ways that would not have been possible back in their homeland.

Third, many missiologists and theologians have been writing about the shift of the center of gravity of Christianity from the Global North to the Global South.[14] We are witnessing a rapid decline of Christianity in the West, with many churches closing or turning into bookstores or pubs because of the lack of

---

12 J. Samuel Escobar, "Mission Fields on the Move," *Christianity Today* 54, no. 5 (May 2010), 28 (my italics).

13 Charlotte Hauswedell, "German Churches See Rise in Baptisms for Refugees," in Germany Guide For Refugees, *Deutsche Welle*, September 5, 2017, http://www.dw.com/en/german-churches-see-rise-in-baptisms-for-refugees/a-38771600 (accessed December 20, 2017).

14 Philip Jenkins, *The Next Christendom: The Coming of Global Christianity* (Oxford: OUP, 2011).

attendees. Nonetheless, since the refugee crisis many Syrian and Iraqi converts have formed new congregations in those nearly dying churches. *The Guardian* reported that European churches have a "growing flock of Muslim refugees," citing as one example a congregation in a Berlin suburb that grew from 150 to almost 700 members in two years due to Muslim converts.[15] The impact of such conversions and revivals in Western churches cannot be dismissed. These new converts are in a unique position to revitalize Christianity in the Western world.

Fourth, the new believers maintain connections to their ancestral lands and carry spiritual burdens for their extended families, communities, and nations. They are a significant mission force who could have a major impact on the entire Islamic world unlike anything we have ever seen. With their linguistic and cultural affinity, in addition to transnational diasporic linkages, they will have a major catalytic influence for gospel penetration across the Middle East and North Africa. The churches in the West must recognize this potential and come alongside of new refugee diaspora believers and churches in order to mobilize them for a major kingdom impact in the region.

Lastly, there are new opportunities for the Western church to build partnerships with the Arab Christians who are already in Europe and North America, as well as those in the Middle East. The trend of reverse mission, where non-Western missionaries send missionaries to Europe and North America, is evident all across Europe; and some of the most effective refugee work is led by Arab believers who hail from Egypt, Jordan, Lebanon, Palestine, etc. The Western church must partner with Arab and African Christians to equip and empower leaders of refugee ministries in the Islamic world and diaspora Muslim communities. They have many advantages to be successful in ministry with refugees and Muslims because they speak the same language, have similar worldviews, and are familiar with the Islamic culture and religion.

The church has a responsibility to be a faithful agent of God's mission, and the current refugee crisis poses a significant opportunity to engage with the unreached people groups who are closer to the gospel as a result of forced displacement. Many who were hostile to Christianity and had a distorted view of it are open to hear and accept the good news in a diasporic refugee setting. Christians worldwide must embrace a biblical mandate regarding refugees and embrace the missionary work among and through refugees, because God is sovereign over all human dispersion and is doing a new work among refugees everywhere.

---

15 Harriet Sherwood and Philip Oltermann, "European Churches Say Growing Flock Of Muslim Refugees Are Converting," *The Guardian*, June 5, 2016, https://www.theguardian.com/world/2016/jun/05/european-churches-growing-flock-muslim-refugees-converting-christianity (accessed December 22, 2017).

chapter twenty-two

Conclusion: A Place Called Home

MIRIAM ADENEY, PhD

"Do I dare get on that boat?" Sina groaned. Nine months pregnant, she stood on the shore of Turkey and strained her eyes toward Greece.

As for the boat—dirty, low in the water, with old wooden slats as sideboards—it did not inspire trust. Other boats had sunk. Unscrupulous and callous boat handlers had jettisoned their human cargo when conditions got rough. Sina looked at the scruffy man who harshly urged her to board. He did not inspire trust either. She looked at the angry surf and sharp rocks. She smelled brine and the sweat of human bodies. Suppose she went into labor and gave birth on this open boat, where people were being packed so tightly that no one could lie down?

For months Sina had been clinging to life by her fingertips. Her story is recounted in *Cast Away: True Stories of Survival from Europe's Refugee Crisis*.[1] Born in Eritrea in Africa, Sina and her young husband, Dani, were assigned by a dictatorial government to work in regions far apart from each other. Dani was forced into the military, a highly dangerous job. Then, because of a Bible study in his hostel, orders went out for Dani's arrest. In jail, he would languish. With Sina newly pregnant, he decided that they should flee the country. "Let's just leave everything!" he said.

So they did. Borrowing as much as they could from supportive family and friends, they scrambled across borders, first to Khartoum in Sudan, then through South Sudan, and finally to Uganda—always seeking safety, housing,

---

1 Charlotte McDonald-Gibson, *Cast Away: True Stories of Survival from Europe's Refugee Crisis* (London: Portobello Books, 2016).

visas, and tickets to take them further from the Eritrean secret service. In Uganda, after paying $14,000 for visas and tickets to Turkey, Dani was betrayed by a travel broker and detained. But Sina remained free. She must go on, Dani insisted. He would join her later. So Sina, although she was eight months pregnant, got on a plane and flew to Turkey.

After a few weeks, she was asking herself, "How could I survive here with a new baby? And look, there is Europe just across the sea."

Now the boatman was ready to cast off. As Sina hesitated, he scowled.

"Do I dare *not* to get on board?" she asked herself.

CENTERED, ACTIVE, AND BLESSED

Global flows of people are pouring across the world. This is the context for Sina's journey, to which we will return. At this moment, over 250 million people live outside the countries in which they were born, and another 65 million have been displaced forcibly. Catastrophes, persecutions, and economic collapses push refugees across boundaries. A digital divide and economic inequity scatter the labor force all over the world. Pulsing minds of the next generation and opportunity for a better life push students outward. The focus of this book is refugees, who are defined by the United Nations in specific terms, as noted in the introduction.

In reality, however, refugees are spurred by a complex continuum of motives. Brokenness, corruption, betrayal, ecological loss, and basic stupidity swirl around us—as do beauty, kindness, nobility, and creativity. When we see refugees like Sina suffer, we long for our world to be healed. We groan, along with all of creation, as Paul describes it in Romans 8. "The whole creation groans and waits," yearning for something to energize us to blossom in beauty.

Yet the dizzying kaleidoscope of this world is not the whole picture. At the heart there is a center. Ephesians 1:8–10 speaks of the ultimate mystery of the ages—that God will bring all things in the cosmos together in Christ. This is the center. God hears our groans, and from his eternal center he is drawing all peoples and all dimensions of life together, smoothing the sharp edges, weaving a pattern out of the fragments, developing a harmonious symphony, cultivating a flourishing ecosystem where every refugee can be sheltered, where every migrant can find a place. In Christ, everything in the cosmos is being knit together.

This is the mystery at the heart of the universe. And although it is unfathomably large and incomprehensibly complex, it is also personal. In God's grand unity,

Sina does not lose what makes her unique. Individual persons have a purpose, according to Ephesians 1:12, and that is to live for the praise of God's glory. We are not just statistics, victims, consumers, or producers. We have a sacred calling, a vocation, an anointing—to live with all of our gifts and quirks for the glory of God. Refugees are not just marginal persons. They can connect with the center and experience empowerment to pour out their life's energies loving their neighbors and working toward the Kingdom of God.

Like the rest of us, they are called to action because God is not static. He is not quiet. God is a mover. He acts. He is at work in the world. Most gloriously he moved when the Word became flesh, took on the form of a human being, and humbled himself to the point of death—and then exploded right out of the tomb because God is God over death as well as life. Such a God is not still. No, he moves—because he loves.

The normal Christian life follows this model. Christians move across borders to spread the glory of God. Sometimes this movement is not planned. Abraham was called to leave his homeland and become a nomad. Joseph and Jacob moved to Egypt under duress. Moses fled from Egypt. David hid out among the Philistines and in the desert. Daniel, Esther, Jeremiah, Ezekiel, and Nehemiah lived in exile, and from that displacement gave us great books of Scripture. Philip and other Christians were scattered by persecution. Later Peter dedicated his writing to those dispersed believers. John was exiled on an island. Even Mary and Joseph and Jesus had to escape across a border and become refugees in Egypt. Living outside our birthplace is a common human experience, and God's people are not exempt from it.

While unplanned displacement brings losses, it also can have positive effects. A good portion of the Bible was written from foreign locations. As historian Philip Jenkins says, "Perhaps the exile that initially seems a nightmare may form part of a greater plan, as dispossessed believers carry their witness to other lands. You cannot read the Bible without realizing how the Exile and Diaspora experience could powerfully spread faith into distant corners of the world."[2]

Displacements can bring non-Christians into contact with the gospel and with loving Christian communities, sometimes for the first time. Displacements can drop a new mission field right into a neighborhood of comfortably settled Christians. Displacements can introduce believers of wildly different backgrounds to each other, where each can learn from the other. Displacements can uproot our false sense of security until we have to sink our roots deeper into God. There is much pain in displacement, but there are also blessings.

---

2 Philip Jenkins, "Is this the end for Mideast Christianity" *Christianity Today* Nov 4, 2014. https://www.christianitytoday.com/ct/2014/november/on-edge-of-extinction.html (accessed July 1, 2018)

The Lausanne Occasional Paper 5 (LOP5)—*Christian Witness to Refugees*[3]—delineates a theological framework for responding to the refugee situation, followed by many strategic steps for minimizing losses and maximizing blessings, and emphasizing what local churches can do. Refugee mission fits well within the framework of diaspora missiology, as articulated in the "Seoul Declaration on Diaspora Missiology"[4] and developed more fully in the global compendium *Scattered and Gathered.*[5] Using diaspora missiology framework, refugee ministries can be categorized as mission to refugees, mission through refugees, and mission beyond refugees. All are illustrated in this book.

REFUGEES' NEEDS AND CITIZENS' NEEDS

Depending on refugees' locale, they may be served by local churches and voluntary agencies, or by national government personnel, or by UNHCR, or by international NGOs, including mission agencies. In each region, some of these groups will form partnerships, with each body responsible for certain services. Where governments and economies are strong, local entities will lead, while international bodies will pioneer in poorer and weaker contexts like Somalia. Some countries require refugees to live in camps, but others do not. In many regions of the world, refugees have to fend for themselves. Finally, beyond all the formal agencies is simple neighborliness. This human kindness helps refugees immensely. Some governments, such as Canada's, facilitate such grassroots connections.

After food and shelter, refugees often need help with government forms, language learning, health care, and schooling. Many refugees would like to work and earn incomes. They want to know how to get around and how to act appropriately in their new environment. They want access to media through which they can stay in touch with friends and relatives. They would like to live where they can worship, and where they can conduct festivals, marriages, births, and funerals. They would like protection from criminal elements inside and outside the refugee community. While the two million women who have been raped in Congo need trauma healing, in fact, most refugees have experienced some trauma and could use counseling. Fun and games are important for children and youth, such as those in the Rohingya refugee camps, where 30 percent are reported as being under the age of five.

---

3   *Christian Witness to Refugees*, Lausanne Occasional Paper 5, Report of the Consultation on World Evangelization, June 1980, https://www.lausanne.org/content/lop/lop-5 (accessed March 1, 2018).
4   "Seoul Declaration on Diaspora Missiology," Lausanne Diaspora Educators Consultation, November 11–14, 2009, https://www.lausanne.org/content/statement/the-seoul-declaration-on-diaspora-missiology (accessed March 1, 2018).
5   Sadiri Joy Tira and Tetsunao Yamamori, *Scattered and Gathered: A Global Compendium on Diaspora Missiology* (Oxford: Regnum Press, 2016).

But what about the needs of ordinary citizens who live in the countries to which refugees come? This question arises when citizens are urged to help refugees. Four objections recur. First, refugees sometimes break the law by crossing borders illegally and skirting other regulations. Second, refugees consume scarce resources, as in Lebanon where nearly one-third of the population are refugees. There refugees overwhelm water and electrical systems, schools, and even roads—none of which were designed to support a population of this size. Third, when enough refugees introduce another culture, religion, or language, the local people's culture may be changed and they may lose a way of life that is dear to them. Fourth, some citizens themselves need food, shelter, jobs, and trauma healing. Don't we have an obligation to meet those needs first?

These objections deserve a hearing. Take the concern about the law. Law matters. We must be able to trust people to tell the truth and honor agreements. Otherwise, our society will fall apart. We also need secure borders. New people are welcome but must be integrated in ways that increase *shalom* in our communities.

Yet human laws are not eternal. Some immigration laws are flawed and need to be changed. Keeping the law must be balanced with other truths and values. At the practical level, compassionate investigation may reveal that some boundary-crossers would face persecution if they were sent back. Other undocumented arrivals may have begun legal residency processes in good faith but lost papers along the way. This is not uncommon during hectic flights.

However, other immigrants do merit deportation. Empathetic accompaniment can smooth this process. Ministry in the 1,500-bed Northwest Federal Detention Center in Tacoma, Washington, exhibits this. Here, as potential deportees come to faith and are discipled, some go home to plant churches. Volunteers may write to them, visit them in their receiving country, and even nurture supportive Christian networks there.

What about the concern that an influx of refugees may cause us to lose our own culture? This, too, deserves attention. Heritage is precious. As travel writer Pico Ayer says in *Global Soul*, "Scattered as we are across the planet, in the absence of any center at all, people find themselves with a porous sense of self. . . . We are lost . . . in the labyrinth of impersonal spaces."[6] We need roots. Our own people and peoplehood matter. The place where we were born, where our family may have lived for generations, is a treasure. This particular culture and its lifeways enrich the mosaic of God's world. They should not be lost.

Yet even as we value our people's tradition and place, we must also think outside the box—the box of a single country's boundaries. In fact, people have been crossing such boundaries for millennia. Both "push" and "pull" pressures

6 Pico Ayer, *The Global Soul: Jet Lag, Shopping Malls, and the Search for Home.* New York: Alfred Knopf, 2000, 36.

are responsible. Violence, natural disasters, and plain poverty push people to move. And the lure of a journey pulls people, especially young people. They glimpse new opportunities. They seek a quest. Our own ancestors may have overrun existing cultures on the very land that we now claim. So while our culture is precious and should be nurtured and cultivated, there is also room for other cultural traditions. Refugees do pose problems for receiving communities, but these problems are not insuperable. They can be tackled with love and wisdom.

BEST PRACTICES FOR WITNESS

Refugees need nothing more than they need the gospel. God's love, God's empowering, and God's truth are overwhelmingly good benefits. These will ease refugees' days, strengthen their weary spirits, and comfort their aching hearts. Sometimes, however, local traditions or government regulations limit Christian witness.

As always, tact and respect are essential. In the end, however, Christian witness cannot be squelched. The joy of the Lord shining in a glowing face or the patience of persistent friendship will provoke questions about motivation and empowering. witness will occur, even if host Christians don't initiate it.

It may be the least offensive to begin among nominal Christian refugees, such as Iraqi refugees in Jordan. In all cases, Bibles, New Testaments, and gospel portions in the appropriate languages should be stockpiled and accessible to any local who wants to witness. As well, there should be copies of the *Jesus video* in those languages and dialects, and information on appropriate internet sites. Workers from some countries may have language skills and cultural ties that connect better than others. They should be encouraged and equipped. Song is another useful practice. Softly singing or playing well-selected lyrics can stimulate questions about faith.

There are many models for multicultural churches, some with separate-language worship services and others with intermingled worship. Youth discipleship deserves high priority, especially when children are growing up in places where they will have no hope of becoming citizens. Helping leaders and laity get theological education is important too. Sometimes former refugees who have migrated to freer, richer nations will return periodically to teach Bible.

If a "difficult access" nation prohibits witness, there are probably members of that people group scattered across the globe. Some of them may have become Christians. It is worth searching them out to share prayer and knowledge and language-appropriate resources. This can strengthen everyone, so that rather than "reinventing the wheel" separately, concerned Christians can build on each other's strengths and go further and higher and broader and deeper faster.

WORKERS CAN BURN OUT

Finally, those who serve refugees have needs. Counselors speak of burnout, compassion fatigue, and the transference of trauma. When responsible workers face a flood of needs, it is easy to neglect time with God, time with one's spouse, or time for sleep. Such workers may become chronically exhausted, hypervigilant, unable to listen well, and unable to embrace complexity. Cognitive changes can result. To guard against these dangers, workers must cultivate friends, social support, and religious support. They must set boundaries, including boundaries for media and for quiet time. They must give themselves space to feel pain.

If possible, even amid overwhelming paradoxes, they must seek to make meaning out of their situation. Bathing in Scripture will help. On one hand, they can identify with many biblical people who faced incomprehensible circumstances, like Habakkuk. On the other hand, they are reminded that God himself entered human pain deeply through the incarnation and the crucifixion. And God ultimately will overwhelm all that causes tragedies, and will invite them into a glorious kingdom. Meanwhile, they can receive daily grace and empowerment to serve human needs, following God's own example.

IS THERE ANY SAFE PLACE?

When Sina, the pregnant Eritrean, debated whether to board a boat to Greece, she was seeking a secure place. Did she get on the boat? She did. Then, just as she had feared, the boat crashed on rocks and broke into pieces. However, this happened in sight of the Greek shoreline. A Greek man swam out and rescued her. She went directly to the hospital and gave birth to a healthy boy, whom she named Andonis in honor of her rescuer.

Ultimately, Sina would carry Andonis through seven European countries during his first year, from Greece to Macedonia to Serbia to Hungary to Germany to Austria and eventually to Sweden. For most of these border-crossings she paid smugglers. Sometimes a group of refugees would walk for six or eight hours. She would have to run ahead in order to sit and nurse her baby or change his diapers. Then she would have to run to catch up with the group. On very long walks she worried that she was not carrying enough water and food to sustain her milk supply. Sometimes she had to spend the night sitting on the cement outside a police station. Once she and her baby were deposited with two Somali men at three a.m. in a parking lot in pouring rain. Another time, when the refugees were cowering on the ground to avoid Hungarian police, the smuggler came along with an injection and said, "We have medicine for children to keep them quiet." All the refugees wanted her to allow Andonis to receive the shot, but Sina stood her ground and refused. When she finally arrived in Austria and told the officials that she wanted to go on to Germany, they drove her back to a police station in Hungary. Along the way Sina had to come to terms with the news that her beloved husband Dani had died of malaria back in Africa, and would never see or hold his son. Now Sina is raising their child alone in Sweden, where she has claimed asylum.

Like Sina, millions of refugees are scrambling to find a secure place. In our biblical heritage, Moses bounced from the slave shack to the palace to the alien family to the shepherd's tent to forty years in the wilderness—not to mention the basket in the bulrushes. In spite of all that displacement, Moses found a secure place. Psalm 90, which is attributed to him, says that beyond all of Moses' shifting circumstances there was a settled center. The psalm opens with the words, "Lord, you have been our dwelling place throughout all generations" (NIV).

David, too, longed for a secure place, especially when he was on the run. His Psalm 91 speaks of snares, pestilence, terror, weapons, plague, darkness, and stalking. He yearned for a refuge, a secure dwelling place, a safe tent. Yet years before he became king, David, like Moses, had found a safe place. Even in the context of all the threats, Psalm 91 begins with the words, "Whoever dwells in the shelter of the Most High will rest in the shadow of the Almighty."

There is indeed a safe place, and it is one that is available to every refugee.

RECOMMENDED READING

Adeney, Miriam and Sadiri J. Tira, *Wealth, Women and God: How to Flourish Spiritually and Economically in Tough Places*, Pasadena, CA: William Carey Library, 2015.

Bala, Sharon. *The Boat People*. New York: Alfred A. Knof, 2018.

Bauman, Stephan, Matthew Soerens, and Issam Smeir, *Seeking Refuge: On the Shores of the Global Refugee Crisis,* Moody Press, 2016.

Carroll, Daniel R.M. *Christians at the Borders: Immigration, the Church and the Border,* Grand Rapids: Brazos Press, 2013.

Christianity Today, "Responding to the Refugee Crisis," July 2017.

Kaemingk, Matthew. *Christian Hospitality and Muslim Immigration in an Age of Fear*, Grand Rapids: William B. Eerdmans, 2018.

Keifert, Patrick R. *Welcoming the Stranger: A Public Theology of Worship and Evangelism* Minneapolis: Fortress Press, 1992.

Kingsley, Patrick. *The New Odyssey: The Story of Europe's Refugee Crisis,* Norton & Co, 2017.

Mayfield, Danielle L. *Assimilate or Go Home: Notes from a Failed Missionary on Rediscovering Faith*, San Francisco, HarperOne, 2016.

McDonald-Gibson, Charlotte. *Cast Away: True Stories of Survival from Europe's Refugee Crisis*. London: Portobello Books, 2016.

Myers, Ched and Matthew Colwell, *Our God is Undocumented: Biblical Faith and Immigrant Justice,* Marynoll, NY: Orbis Books, 2012.

Newman, Elizabeth. *Untamed Hospitality: Welcoming God and Other Strangers,* Grand Rapids: Brazos Press, 2007

Payne, J. D. *Strangers Next Door: Immigration, Migration, and Mission,* Downers Grove: IVP, 2012.

Pohl, Christine. *Making Room: Recovering Hospitality as a Christian Tradition,* Grand Rapids: W.B. Eerdmans, 1999.

Sorens, Matthew and Jenny Yang, *Welcoming the Stranger: Justice, Compassion and Truth in Immigration Debate,* Downers Grove, IL: IVP Books, 2009.

Sutherland, Arthur. *I Was a Stranger: Christian Theology of Hospitality, Nashville,* Abingdon Press, 2006.

Tira, Sadiri Joy and Tetsunao Yamamori, *Scattered and Gathered: Global Compendium on Diaspora Missiology,* Oxford: Regnum Books, 2016.

REFUGEE HIGHWAY PARTNERSHIP

The Refugee Highway Partnership (RHP) began out of a historic consultation October 2001 in Izmir, Turkey—the first ever global gathering on Christian refugee ministry. The consultation, sponsored by the World Evangelical Alliance, was held under the title Bringing Hope to the Refugee Highway. Nearly 175 leaders from every global region attended and explored how they could do things together that they were not able to do by themselves. As a direct result of this consultation, the Refugee Highway Partnership was set up as a network and established this purpose statement:

> Because of our God-inspired love for refugees, and the biblical mandate to care for the alien, and because of our conviction that we can do this best by collaborating; the Refugee Highway Partnership (RHP) seeks to create and build a community that a) Facilitates more effective ministry, b) Stimulates strategic initiatives and c) Envisions and equips the church so that refugee ministries are strengthened, and more refugees are served.

Core values of the RHP include: a commitment to local church engagement; belief that forcibly displaced people themselves are a primary asset and our partners in refugee ministry; dedication to partnering and collaboration; responsibility to the welfare of refugee workers; and a commitment to holistic ministry—responding to the physical, emotional, and spiritual needs.

Currently, the RHP has regional efforts and held Roundtable leadership gatherings in: Africa, Brazil, Europe, the Middle East, North America, South Asia, and Turkey. Emerging regional initiatives are currently taking place in South East Asia and Oceania. In addition, the RHP has issue-based focus groups addressing Children and Youth, Trafficking, Discipleship, Prayer, Refugee Churches, and Advocacy.

Since 2008, the RHP has sponsored World Refugee Sunday each June helping to mobilize the church in being aware of the global challenge of the forcibly displaced and establishing designated time praying for them.

For more information, see: **www.RefugeeHighway.net**

GLOBAL DIASPORA NETWORK

An issue network of the

Lausanne Movement

Fulfilling God's Redemptive Mission for the People on the Move

Vision: To empower the global church and respond effectively to the missional opportunities arising out of global migration and diaspora communities worldwide.

Our Mandate:

1. To catalyze the global Church to demonstrate and proclaim the whole gospel to, through, and beyond diasporas everywhere.

2. To foster theological thinking on diaspora through dialogues and consultations with reflective practitioners and scholars for the development of relevant resources.

3. To network with local churches, denominations, mission agencies, NGOs, theological institutions, and other mission networks.

4. To accelerate the development and adoption of diaspora missiology in leading seminaries, universities, and institutions worldwide.

Contact:

4th Floor Back to the Bible Bldg. 135 West Avenue,
Quezon City, Philippines 1104
Phone: +632 788 24 02   Email: info@global-diaspora.com
www.Global-Diaspora.com